KT-570-200

RUDYARD KIPLING was born in Bombay in 1865. After schooling in England he returned to India in 1882 to work as a journalist and it was here that he published his early stories and verse. Leaving India in 1889 for London, he became an overnight literary success and remained a celebrity, if at times a notorious one, for the rest of his life. From the late 1890s his work was often associated with British Imperialism and this (somewhat unfairly) tended to colour its reception. He married Caroline Balestier in 1892 and they had three children, of whom only one survived him. Kipling died in 1936.

HARRY RICKETTS was born in London and after graduating from Oxford taught at Hong Kong University and Leicester University. His publications include: a collection of Hong Kong stories, *People Like Us* (1977); an edition of Kipling's 'lost' New Zealand story, 'One Lady at Wairakei' (1983); a book of interviews with New Zealand poets, *Talking About Ourselves* (1986) and a number of articles on Kipling's work. He is married with six children and at present lives in Wellington, New Zealand where he is a Senior Lecturer in the English Department at Victoria University.

For Tom

KIPLING'S LOST WORLD

Edited and with an Introduction

by

Harry Ricketts

TABB HOUSE

KINGSTON UPON THAMES
PUBLIC LIBRARIES

C72073

ALL	CLASS
M	828
CAT	REF
P	
495	

Published by Tabb House 1989
7 Church Street, Padstow, Cornwall, PL28 8BG

Introduction and other editorial matter © Harry Ricketts, 1989

Paperback ISBN 0907018 71 8
Hardback ISBN 0907018 76 9

This book is sold subject to the condition that it shall not be lent, re-sold, hired out or otherwise circulated without the publisher's consent in any form of bindings or covers other than those in which it is published

Typeset by St. George Typesetting, Redruth, Cornwall.
Printed by Bookcraft, Midsomer Norton, Bath, Avon

CONTENTS

ACKNOWLEDGEMENTS

I should like to thank Hugh Roberts, David Norton, Vincent O'Sullivan, Caroline White and very particularly David Kynaston and my wife, Rita, for all the time and assistance they have given me in preparing this edition. I am also grateful to the Master and Fellows of Magdalene College, Cambridge, for permission to reproduce their portrait of Rudyard Kipling by William Strang.

INTRODUCTION

AN admiration for Kipling should by now require no apology;
no longer any need to claim you like only *Kim* and the
children's stories. Indeed, the last thirty years have seen a
marked resurgence of interest in him and his work. There
have been four full-length biographies, a shelf of critical books
and since he came out of copyright the recent spate of reissues
and new selections. Kipling's literary reputation it seems is
starting to conform to an almost archetypal pattern: early fame;
subsequent neglect; gradual rehabilitation.

And yet for all this renewed enthusiasm (some due no doubt
to post-Raj nostalgia), many aspects of Kipling's hugely varied
output remain ignored and unexplored. The present collection
of stories, poems and speeches offers the reader an opportunity
to encounter one of these 'lost' Kiplings: the Kipling who
wrote with great originality and insight about literature, about
the sources of inspiration, about the nature of his own art.

Why is this 'literary' Kipling so little known? The reason I
think is obvious enough: only very recently has he begun to be
taken seriously *as a writer*. For decades the image of Kipling
as the self-appointed mouthpiece of British Imperialism was
so instilled, so overpowering, that other areas of his work were
simply invisible.

Kipling himself must of course take some of the blame for
this. Throughout his career he had a tendency to play down
his own intense literariness in the face of an audience that
above all valued those who 'did' things. He knew that what
overworked District Officers, soldiers or construction engineers
expected from him was an accurate depiction of their jobs and
the conditions under which they performed them; what they
did not expect was literature. Kipling's response to this was
thoroughly characteristic. He duly told them stories about their

lives, packed with realistic detail, but shadowed these stories with literary archetypes that unobtrusively extend the world of the stories while at the same time satisfying his own imaginative needs. So, behind 'Beyond the Pale' (*Plain Tales from the Hills*) one can sense the story of Abelard and Eloise; behind 'In Flood Time' (*In Black and White*) that of Hero and Leander. These ghostly archetypes also flicker in the background of the children's stories: 'The Pardoner's Tale' behind 'The King's Ankus' (*The Second Jungle Book*); *King Lear* behind 'The Tree of Justice' (*Rewards and Fairies*).

Nor is this the only way that Kipling found of smuggling literature into unexpected and apparently unliterary contexts. He will often use a famous literary allusion at a climactic moment in a story but defamiliarise it so that the allusion is renewed, almost as it were reinvented. There is a notable example of this in 'Love-o'-Women' (*Many Inventions*) where the syphilitic gentleman-ranker Larry Tighe dies, saying to the woman he loved but corrupted, 'I'm dyin', Aigypt – dyin' ' – Antony's words to Cleopatra marvellously recharged in the Irish brogue of Mulvaney who narrates the story but misses its literary frisson. Or there is 'Mrs Bathurst' (*Traffics and Discoveries*), usually considered Kipling's most enigmatic story, where the warrant officer Vickery deserts his ship under mysterious circumstances uttering Hamlet's final words: 'The rest is silence'.

Variations of this covert, literary interplay occur in story after story. By the time of *Debits and Credits* (1926) Kipling had brought the technique to such a point of sophistication that the interplay is also happening between the stories themselves. In that volume one story lights up another and the poems that bracket the stories not only modify them but often the stories that come before and after.

But if Kipling was always extremely adept at camouflaging his literarinesss, what about the stories, poems and speeches in this collection where he gives it full rein, where he is explicitly concerned with literature and literary subjects? The Notes at the end of the volume give specific information and commentary on each item but in general it seems true to say that these

pieces offer a new and surprising Kipling. The six stories
show a Kipling who can by turns be as scholastically inventive
and metafictionally teasing as Borges or Eco ('The Last of
the Stories', "Proofs of Holy Writ") and as psychologically
subtle as Henry James ('Dayspring Mishandled'). And who but
Kipling could have produced a story as original as "Wireless",
where a consumptive chemist's assistant starts to reconstruct
parts of the 'The Eve of St Agnes' (although he has neither
heard of Keats nor read the poem)? Or a story as effortlessly
multi-layered as 'The Bull That Thought', where the surface
narrative about a bull that can think (and the alarming/comic
consequences of this in the bullring) gradually shows itself to
be offering startling self-portraits of the artist as young bull and
the artist as ageing matador?

The poems too present a Kipling considerably at odds with
the received account: the Kipling of 'If-', the thumping
ballads, the jingoistic hymns and the copybook phrases. Here
by contrast is a poet who can raise all kinds of central questions
about what literature is, how it arises, what it can and cannot
hope to encompass; and do all this in a remarkable variety of
voices and modes: from the breezy cheek of 'When 'Omer
Smote 'Is Bloomin' Lyre' to the riddling ironies of 'The
Fabulists'; from the assured Sapphics of 'The Craftsman' to
the quieter, meditative lyricism of 'The Survival'.

And then there is 'A Letter to the *Spectator*' and the two
speeches, 'Literature' and 'Fiction'. 'A Letter to the *Spectator*',
describing how Shakespeare might have got the germ of the
idea and some of the background information for *The Tempest*,
would I think be worth resurrecting simply because it is so little
known. As it is, it also offers by implication a revealing glimpse
of the way Kipling himself went about collecting 'copy'. The two
speeches show Kipling disclosing (sometimes cryptically, always
entertainingly) some of his most deeply-held convictions about
the origins and the value of literature. Through a mixture of
parable and plain statement, he suggests the way in which
literature continues to fulfil a basic tribal need and yet how
for those apparently random few who possess 'the magic
of the necessary word' it is more of an affliction than a

blessing. To which one should perhaps add that on several occasions (particularly in the later 'Fiction') he demonstrates just how little his more respected contemporaries had to teach him about the nuts and bolts of fictional theory. His terminology is certainly different from theirs but he shows that he is equally well-acquainted with the crucially problematic relationship between fiction and truth and clearly no stranger to the ambiguities of authorial intention. Indeed, his claim in 'Fiction' that 'The true nature and intention...of a writer's work does not lie within his own knowledge' anticipates by some years famous pronouncements like T.S. Eliot's in *The Use of Poetry and the Use of Criticism* (1933) where he comments that 'what a poem means is as much what it means to others as what it means to the author'.

Kipling's sense of literature was steeped in the past, in the Classics, the Bible, the Icelandic Sagas, Shakespeare, the great and the minor poets and prose writers; and yet for all that he is also thoroughly modern.

If there is to be a really radical re-evaluation of his work and its enduring significance, then the discovery of the 'literary' Kipling, the Kipling of this collection, provides a crucial starting point.

Harry Ricketts
Wellington, 1989

THE LAST OF THE STORIES

Wherefore I perceive that there is nothing better, than that a man should rejoice in his own works; for that is his portion. – *Ecclesiastes* iii.22.

'KENCH with a long hand, lazy one,' I said to the punkah-coolie. 'But I am tired,' said the coolie.

'Then go to Jehannum and get another man to pull,' I replied, which was rude and, when you come to think of it, unnecessary.

'Happy thought – go to Jehannum!' said a voice at my elbow. I turned and saw, seated on the edge of my bed, a large and luminous Devil.

'I'm not afraid,' I said. 'You're an illusion bred by too much tobacco and not enough sleep. If I look at you steadily for a minute you will disappear. You are an *ignis fatuus*.'

'Fatuous yourself!' answered the Devil blandly. 'Do you mean to say you don't know *me*?' He shrivelled up to the size of a blob of sediment on the end of a pen, and I recognised my old friend the Devil of Discontent, who lives in the bottom of the inkpot, but emerges half a day after each story has been printed with a host of useless suggestions for its betterment.

'Oh, it's you, is it?' I said. 'You're not due till next week. Get back to your inkpot.'

'Hush!' said the Devil. 'I have an idea.'

'Too late, as usual. I know your ways.'

'No. It's a perfectly practicable one. Your swearing at the coolie suggested it. Did you ever hear of a man called Dante? – charmin' fellow, friend o' mine.'

' "Dante once prepared to paint a picture," ' I quoted.

'Yes. I inspired that notion – but never mind. Are you willing to play Dante to my Virgil? I can't guarantee a nine-circle Inferno, any more than *you* can turn out a cantoed epic, but there's absolutely no risk and – it will run to three columns at least.'

'But what sort of Hell do you own?' I said. 'I fancied your operations were mostly above ground. You have no jurisdiction over the dead.'

'Sainted Leopardi!' rapped the Devil, resuming natural size. 'Is *that* all you know? I'm proprietor of one of the largest Hells in existence – the Limbo of Lost Endeavour, where the souls of all the Characters go.'

'Characters? What Characters?'

'All the Characters that are drawn in books, painted in novels, sketched in magazine articles, thumb-nailed in *feuilletons* or in any way created by anybody and everybody who has had the fortune or misfortune to put his or her writings into print.'

'That sounds like a quotation from a prospectus. What do you herd Characters for? Aren't there enough souls in the Universe?'

'Who possess souls and who do not? For aught you can prove, man may be soulless and the creatures he writes about immortal. Anyhow, about a hundred years after printing became an established nuisance, the loose Characters used to blow about Interplanetary Space in legions which interfered with traffic. So they were collected, and their charge became mine by right. Would you care to see them? *Your own are there.*'

'That decides me. But *is* it hotter than Northern India?'

'On my Devildom, no. Put your arms around my neck and sit tight. I'm going to dive!'

He plunged from the bed head-first into the floor. There was a smell of floor-cloth and damp earth; and then fell the black darkness of night.

*   *   *   *   *

WE stood before a door in a topless wall, from the further side of which came faintly the roar of infernal fires.

'But you said there was no danger!' I cried in an extremity of terror.

'No more there is,' said the Devil. 'That's only the Furnace of First Edition. Will you go on? No other human being has set foot here in the flesh. Let me bring the door to your notice. Pretty design, isn't it? A joke of the Master's.'

I shuddered, for the door was nothing more than a coffin, the backboard knocked out, set on end in the thickness of the wall. As I hesitated, the silence of space was cut by a sharp, shrill whistle, like that of a live shell, which rapidly grew louder and louder. 'Get away from the door,' said the Devil of Discontent quickly. 'Here's a Soul coming to its place.' I took refuge under the broad vans of the Devil's wings. The whistle rose to an ear-splitting shriek and a naked Soul flashed past me.

'Always the same,' said the Devil quietly. 'These little writers are so anxious to reach their reward. H'm, I don't think he like *his'n*, though.' A yell of despair reached my ears and I shuddered afresh. 'Who was he?' I asked. 'Hack-writer for a pornographic firm in Belgium, exporting to London – you'll understand presently – and now we'll go in,' said the Devil. 'I must apologise for that creature's rudeness. He should have stopped at the distance-signal for line-clear. You can hear the Souls whistling there now.'

'Are they the souls of men?' I whispered.

'Yes – writer-men. That's why they are so shrill and querulous. Welcome to the Limbo of Lost Endeavour!'

We passed into a domed hall, more vast than visions could embrace, crowded to its limit by men, women, and children. Round the eye of the dome ran, a flickering fire, that terrible quotation from Job: 'Oh, that mine enemy had written a book!'

'Neat, isn't it?' said the Devil, following my glance. 'Another joke of the Master's. Man of *Us*, y'know. In the old days we used to put the Characters into a disused circle of Dante's Inferno, but they grew overcrowded. So Balzac and Théophile Gautier were commissioned to write up this building. It took them three years to complete, and is one of the finest under earth. Don't attempt to describe it unless you are *quite* sure you are equal to Balzac and Gautier in collaboration. Look at the crowds and tell me what you think of them.'

I looked long and earnestly, and saw that many of the multitude were cripples. They walked on their heels or their toes, or with a list to the right or left. A few of them possessed odd eyes and parti-coloured hair; more threw themselves into absurd and impossible attitudes; and every fourth woman seemed to be weeping.

'Who are these?' I said.

'Mainly the population of three-volume novels that never reach the six-shilling stage. See that beautiful girl with one grey eye and one brown, and the black-and-yellow hair? Let her be an awful warning to you how you correct your proofs. She was created by a careless writer a month ago, and he changed all colours in the second volume. So she came here as you see her. There will be trouble when she meets her author. He can't alter her now, and she says she'll accept no apology.'

'But when will she meet her author?'

'That's not in *my* department. Do you notice a general air of expectancy among all the Characters? They are waiting for their authors. Look! That explains the system better than I can.'

A lovely maiden, at whose feet I would willingly have fallen and worshipped, detached herself from the crowd and hastened to the door through which I had just come. There was a prolonged whistle without, a Soul dashed through the coffin and fell upon her neck. The girl with parti-coloured hair eyed the couple enviously as they departed arm-in-arm to the other side of the hall.

'That man,' said the Devil, 'wrote one magazine story, of twenty-four pages, ten years ago when he was desperately in love with a flesh-and-blood woman. He put all his heart into the work, and created the girl you have just seen. The flesh-and-blood woman married some one else and died – it's a way they have – but the man has this girl for his very own, and she will everlastingly grow sweeter.'

'Then the Characters are independent?'

'Slightly! Have you never known one of your Characters – even yours – get beyond control as soon as they are made?'

'That's true. Where are those two happy creatures going?'

'To the Levels. You've heard of authors finding their levels?

We keep all the Levels here. As each writer enters, he picks up his Characters, or they pick *him* up, as the case may be, and to the Levels he goes.'

'I should like to see – '

'So you shall, when you come through that door a second time – whistling. I can't take you there now.'

'Do you only keep the Characters of living scribblers in this hall?'

'We should be crowded out if we didn't draft them off somehow. Step this way and I'll take you to the Master. One moment, though. There's John Ridd with Lorna Doone, and there are Mr Maliphant and the Bormalacks – clannish folk, those Besant Characters – don't let The Twins talk to you about Literature and Art. Come along. What's here?'

The white face of Mr John Oakhurst, gambler, broke through the press. 'I wish to explain,' said he in a level voice, 'that had I been consulted I should never have blown out my brains with the Duchess and all that Poker Flat lot. I wish to add that the only woman I ever loved was the wife of Brown of Calaveras.' He passed his hand behind him suggestively. 'All right, Mr Oakhurst,' I said hastily; 'I believe you.' '*Kin* you set it right?' he asked, dropping into the Doric of the Gulches. I caught a trigger's cloth-muffled click. 'Just Heavens!' I groaned. 'Must I be shot for the sake of another man's Characters?'

Oakhurst levelled his revolver at my head, but the weapon was struck up by the hand of Yuba Bill. 'You durned fool!' said the stage-driver. 'Hevn't I told you no one but a blamed idiot shoots at sight *now*? Let the galoot go. You kin see by his eyes he's no party to your matrimonial arrangements.' Oakhurst retired with an irreproachable bow, but in my haste to escape I fell over Caliban, his head in a melon and his tame orc under his arm. He spat like a wild-cat.

'Manners none, customs beastly,' said the Devil. 'We'll take the Bishop with us. They all respect the Bishop.' And the great Bishop Blougram joined us, calm and smiling, with the news, for my private ear, that Mr Gigadibs despised him no longer.

We were arrested by a knot of semi-nude Bacchantes kissing

a clergyman. The Bishop's eyes twinkled, and I turned to the Devil for explanation.

'That's Robert Elsmere – what's left of him,' said the Devil. 'Those are French *feuilleton* women and scourings of the Opéra Comique. He has been lecturing 'em, and they don't like it.'

'He lectured *me!*' said the Bishop with a bland smile.

'He has been a nuisance ever since he came here. By the Holy Law of Proportion, he had the audacity to talk to the Master! Called him a "pot-bellied barbarian"! That is why he is walking so stiffly now,' said the Devil. 'Listen! Marie Pigeonnier is swearing deathless love to him. On my word, we ought to segregate the French Characters entirely. By the way, your regiment came in very handy for Zola's importations.'

'My regiment?' I said. 'How do you mean?'

'You wrote something about the Tyneside Tail-Twisters, just enough to give the outline of the regiment, and of course it came down here – one thousand and eighty strong. I told it off in hollow squares to pen up the Rougon-Macquart series. There they are.' I looked and saw the Tyneside Tail-Twisters ringing an inferno of struggling, shouting, blaspheming men and women in the costumes of the Second Empire. Now and again the shadowy ranks brought down their butts on the toes of the crowd inside the square, and shrieks of pain followed. 'You should have indicated your men more clearly; they are hardly up to their work,' said the Devil. 'If the Zola tribe increase, I'm afraid I shall have to use up your two companies of the Black Tyrone and two of the Old Regiment.'

'I am proud – ' I began.

'Go slow,' said the Devil. 'You won't be half so proud in a little while, and I don't think much of your regiments, anyway. But they are good enough to fight the French. Can you hear Coupeau raving in the left angle of the square? He used to run about the hall seeing pink snakes, till the children's story-book Characters protested. Come along!'

Never since Caxton pulled his first proof and made for the world a new and most terrible God of Labour had mortal man such an experience as mine when I followed the Devil of Discontent through the shifting crowds below the motto of the

Dome. A few – a very few – of the faces were old friends, but there were thousands whom I did not recognise. Men in every conceivable attire and of every possible nationality, deformed by intention, or the impotence of creation that could not create – blind, unclean, heroic, mad, sinking under the weight of remorse or with eyes made splendid by the light of love and fixed endeavour; women fashioned in ignorance and mourning the errors of their creator, life and thought at variance with body and soul; perfect women such as walk rarely upon this earth, and horrors that were women only because they had not sufficient self-control to be fiends; little children, fair as the morning, who put their hands into mine and made most innocent confidences; loathsome, lank-haired infant-saints, curious as to the welfare of my soul, and delightfully mischievous boys, generalled by the irrepressible Tom Sawyer, who played among murderers, harlots, professional beauties, nuns, Italian bandits, and politicians of state.

The ordered peace of Arthur's Court was broken up by the incursions of Mr John Wellington Wells, and Dagonet, the jester, found that his antics drew no attention so long as the 'dealer in magic and spells,' taking Tristram's harp, sang patter-songs to the Round Table; while a Zulu *impi*, headed by Allan Quatermain, wheeled and shouted in sham fight for the pleasure of Little Lord Fauntleroy. Every century and every type was jumbled in the confusion of one colossal fancy-ball where all the Characters were living their parts.

'Aye, look long,' said the Devil. 'You will never be able to describe it, and the next time you come you won't have the chance. Look long, and look at' – Good's passing with a maiden of the Zu-Vendi must have suggested the idea – 'look at their legs.' I looked, and for the second time noticed the lameness that seemed to be almost universal in the Limbo of Lost Endeavour. Brave men and stalwart to all appearance had one leg shorter than the other; some paced a few inches above the floor, never touching it, and others found the greatest difficulty in preserving their feet at all. The stiffness and laboured gait of these thousands was pitiful to witness. I was sorry for them. I told the Devil as much.

'H'm, said he reflectively, 'that's the world's work. Rather cockeye, ain't it? They do everything but stand on their feet. *You* could improve them, I suppose?' There was an unpleasant sneer in his tone, and I hastened to change the subject.

'I'm tired of walking,' I said. 'I want to see some of my own Characters, and go on to the Master, whoever he may be, afterwards.'

'Reflect,' said the Devil. 'Are you certain – do you know how many they be?'

'No – but I want to see them. That's what I came for.'

'Very well. Don't abuse me if you don't like the view. There are one-and-fifty of your make up to date, and – it's rather an appalling thing to be confronted with fifty-one children. However, here's a special favourite of yours. Go and shake hands with her!'

A limp-jointed, staring-eyed doll was hirpling towards me with a strained smile of recognition. I felt that I knew her only too well – if indeed she were she.

'Keep her off, Devil!' I cried, stepping back. 'I never made *that*!'

' "She began to weep and she began to cry, Lord ha' mercy on me, this is none of I!" You're very rude to – Mrs Hauksbee, and she wants to speak to you,' said the Devil. My face must have betrayed my dismay, for the Devil went on soothingly: 'That's as she is, remember. I *knew* you wouldn't like it. Now what will you give if I make her as she ought to be? No, I don't want your soul, thanks. I have it already, and many others of better quality. Will you, when you write your story, own that I am the best and greatest of all the Devils?' The doll was creeping nearer. 'Yes,' I said hurriedly. 'Anything you like. Only I can't stand her in that state.'

'You'll *have* to when you come next again. Look! No connection with Jekyll and Hyde!' The Devil pointed a lean and inky finger towards the doll, and lo! radiant, bewitching, with a smile of dainty malice, her high heels clicking on the floor like castanets, advanced Mrs Hauksbee as I had imagined her in the beginning.

'Ah!' she said. 'You are here so soon? Not dead yet? That

will come. Meantime, a thousand congratulations. And now, what do you think of me?' She put her hands on her hips, revealed a glimpse of the smallest foot in Simla, and hummed: ' "Just look at that . . . just look at this! And then you'll see I'm not amiss." '

'She'll use exactly the same words when you meet her next time,' said the Devil warningly. 'You dowered her with any amount of vanity, if you left out – Excuse me a minute! I'll fetch up the rest of your menagerie.' But I was looking at Mrs Hauksbee.

'Well?' she said. '*Am* I what you expected?'

I forgot the Devil and all his works, forgot that this was not the woman I had made, and could only murmur rapturously: 'By Jove! You *are* a beauty.' Then, incautiously: 'And you stand on your feet!'

'Good Heavens!' said Mrs Hauksbee. 'Would you, at my time of life, have me stand on my head?' She folded her arms and looked me up and down.

I was grinning imbecilely – the woman was so alive. 'Talk,' I said absently; 'I want to hear you talk.'

'I am not used to being spoken to like a coolie,' she replied.

'Never mind,' I said. 'That may be for outsiders, but I made you and I've a right – '

'You have a right? You made me? My dear sir, if I didn't know that we should bore each other so inextinguishably hereafter I should read you an hour's lecture this instant. You made me! I suppose you will have the audacity to pretend that you understand me – that you *ever* understood me. Oh, man, man – foolish man! If you only knew!'

'Is that the person who thinks he understands us, Loo?' drawled a voice at her elbow. The Devil had returned with a cloud of witnesses, and it was Mrs Mallowe who was speaking.

'I've touched 'em all up,' said the Devil in an aside. 'You couldn't stand 'em raw. But don't run away with the notion that they are your work. I show you what they ought to be. You must find out for yourself how to make 'em so.'

'Am I allowed to remodel the batch – up above?' I asked anxiously.

'*Litera scripta manet*. That's in the Delectus and Eternity.'
He turned round to the semicircle of Characters: 'Ladies and
gentlemen, who are all a great deal better than you should be
by virtue of *my* power, let me introduce you to your maker. If
you have anything to say to him, you can say it.'

'What insolence!' said Mrs Hauksbee between her teeth.
'This isn't a Peterhof drawing-room. I haven't the slightest
intention of being leveed by this person. Polly, come here and
we'll watch the animals go by.' She and Mrs Mallowe stood at
my side. I turned crimson with shame, for it is an awful thing
to see one's Characters in the solid.

'Wal,' said Gilead P. Beck as he passed, 'I would not be
you at this *pre*-cise moment of time, not for all the ile in
the univarsal airth. *No*, sirr! I thought my dinner-party was
soul-shatterin', but it's mush – mush and milk – to your circus.
Let the good work go on!'

I turned to the company and saw that they were men and
women, standing upon their feet as folks should stand. Again I
forgot the Devil, who stood apart and sneered. From the distant
door of entry I could hear the whistle of arriving Souls, from
the semi-darkness at the end of the hall came the thunderous
roar of the Furnace of First Edition, and everywhere the restless
crowds of Characters muttered and rustled like wind-blown
autumn leaves. But I looked upon my own people and was
perfectly content as man could be.

'I have seen you study a new dress with just such an
expression of idiotic beatitude,' whispered Mrs Mallowe to Mrs
Hauksbee. 'Hush!' said the latter. 'He thinks he understands.'
Then to me: 'Please trot them out. Eternity is long enough in
all conscience, but that is no reason for wasting it. *Pro*-ceed, or
shall I call them up? Mrs Vansuythen, Mr Boulte, Mrs Boulte,
Captain Kurrell, and the Major!'

The European population in Kashima in the Dosehri hills,
the actors in the Wayside Comedy, moved towards me; and I
saw with delight that they were human. 'So you wrote about
us?' said Mrs Boulte. 'About my confession to my husband and
my hatred of that Vansuythen woman? Did you think that you
understood? Are *all* men such fools?'

'That woman is bad form,' said Mrs Hauksbee, 'but she speaks the truth. I wonder what these soldiers have to say.' Gunner Barnabas and Private Shacklock stopped, saluted, and hoped I would take no offence if they gave it as their opinion that I had not 'got them down quite right.' I gasped.

A spurred Hussar succeeded, his wife on his arm. It was Captain Gadsby and Minnie, and close behind them swaggered Jack Mafflin, the Brigadier-General in his arms. 'Had the cheek to try to describe our life, had you?' said Gadsby carelessly. 'Ha-hmm! S'pose he understood, Minnie?' Mrs Gadsby raised her face to her husband and murmured: 'I'm *sure* he didn't Pip,' while Poor Dear Mamma, still in her riding-habit, hissed: 'I'm sure he didn't understand *me*.' And these also went their way.

One after another they filed by – Trewinnard, the pet of his Department; Otis Yeere, lean and lanthorn-jawed; Crook O'Neil and Bobby Wick arm in arm; Janki Meah, the blind miner in the Jimahari coal-fields; Afzul Khan, the policeman; the murderous Pathan horse-dealer, Durga Dass; the *bunnia*; Boh Da Thone, the dacoit; Dana Da, weaver of false magic; the Leander of the Barwhi ford; Peg Barney, drunk as a coot; Mrs Delville, the dowd; Dinah Shadd, large, red-cheeked and resolute; Simmons, Slane and Losson; Georgie Porgie and his Burmese helpmate; a shadow in a high collar, who was all that I had ever indicated of the Hawley Boy – the nameless men and women who had trod the Hill of Illusion and lived in the Tents of Kedar, and last, His Majesty the King.

Each one in passing told me the same tale, and the burden thereof was: 'You did not understand.' My heart turned sick within me. 'Where's Wee Willie Winkie?' I shouted. 'Little children don't lie.'

A clatter of pony's feet followed, and the child appeared, habited as on the day he rode into Afghan territory to warn Coppy's love against the 'bad men.' 'I've been playing,' he sobbed, 'playing on ve Levels wiv Jackanapes and Lollo, an' *he* says I'm only just borrowed. I *isn't* borrowed. I'm Willie Wi-*inkie*! Vere's Coppy?'

' "Out of the mouths of babes and sucklings," ' whispered

the Devil, who had drawn nearer. 'You know the rest of the proverb. Don't look as if you were going to be shot in the morning! Here are the last of your gang.'

I turned despairingly to the Three Musketeers, dearest of all my children to me – to Private Mulvaney, Ortheris, and Learoyd. Surely the Three would not turn against me as the others had done! I shook hands with Mulvaney. 'Terence, how goes? Are *you* going to make fun of me, too?'

''Tis not for me to make fun av you, sorr,' said the Irishman, 'knowin' as I *du* know fwhat good frinds we've been for the matther av three years.'

'Fower,' said Ortheris. ''Twas in the Helanthami barricks, H block, we was become acquaint, an' 'ere's thankin' you kindly for all the beer we've drunk twix' that and now.'

'Four ut is, then,' said Mulvaney. 'He an' Dinah Shadd are your frinds, but – ' He stood uneasily.

'But what?' I said.

'Savin' your presince, sorr, an' it's more than onwillin' I am to be hurtin' you; you did not ondhersthand. On my sowl an' honour, sorr, you did not ondhersthand. Come along, you two.'

But Ortheris stayed for a moment to whisper: 'It's Gawd's own trewth, but there's this 'ere to think. 'Tain't the bloomin' belt that's wrong, as Peg Barney sez, when he's up for bein' dirty on p'rade. 'Tain't the bloomin' belt, sir; it's the bloomin' pipeclay.' Ere I could seek an explanation he had joined his companions.

'For a private soldier, a singularly shrewd man,' said Mrs. Hauksbee, and she repeated Ortheris's words. The last drop filled my cup, and I am ashamed to say that I bade her be quiet in a wholly unjustifiable tone. I was rewarded by what would have been a notable lecture on propriety, had I not said to the Devil: 'Change that woman to a d – d doll again! Change 'em all back as they were – as they are. I'm sick of them.'

'Poor wretch!' said the Devil of Discontent very quietly. 'They are changed.'

The reproof died on Mrs Hauksbee's lips, and she moved away marionette-fashion, Mrs Mallowe trailing after her. I hastened after the remainder of the Characters, and they were changed indeed – even as the Devil had said, who kept at my side.

They limped and stuttered and staggered and mouthed and staggered round me, till I could endure no more.

'So I am the master of this idiotic puppet-show, am I?' I said bitterly, watching Mulvaney trying to come to attention by spasms.

'*In saecula saeculorum,*' said the Devil, bowing his head; 'and you needn't kick, my dear fellow, because they will concern no one but yourself by the time you whistle up to the door. Stop reviling me and uncover. Here's the Master.'

Uncover! I would have dropped on my knees, had not the Devil prevented me, at sight of the portly form of Maître François Rabelais, sometime Curé of Meudon. He wore a smoke-stained apron of the colours of Gargantua. I made a sign which was duly returned. 'An Entered Apprentice in difficulties with his rough ashlar, Worshipful Sir,' explained the Devil. I was too angry to speak.

Said the Master, rubbing his chin: 'Are those things yours?'

'Even so, Worshipful Sir,' I muttered, praying inwardly that the Characters would at least keep quiet while the Master was near.

He touched one or two thoughtfully, put his hand upon my shoulder and started. 'By the Great Bells of Notre Dame, you are in the flesh – the warm flesh! – the flesh I quitted so long – ah, so long! And you fret and behave unseemly because of these shadows! Listen now! I, even I, would give my Three, Panurge, Gargantua, and Pantagruel, for one little hour of the life that is in you. And *I* am the Master!'

But the words gave me no comfort. I could hear Mrs Mallowe's joints cracking – or it might have been merely her stays.

'Worshipful Sir, he will not believe that,' said the Devil. 'Who live by shadows lust for shadows. Tell him something more to his need.'

The Master grunted contemptuously: 'And he is flesh and blood! Know this, then. The First Law is to make them stand upon their feet, and the Second is to make them stand upon their feet, and the Third is to make them stand upon their feet. But, for all that, Trajan is a fisher of frogs.' He passed on, and I could hear him say to himself: 'One hour – one minute – of life in the flesh, and I would sell the Great Perhaps thrice over!'

'Well,' said the Devil, 'you've made the Master angry, seen about all there is to be seen, except the Furnace of First Edition, and, as the Master is in charge of that, I should avoid it. Now you'd better go. You know what you ought to do?'

'I don't need all Hell – '

'Pardon me. Better men than you have called this Paradise.'

'All *Hell*,' I said, 'and the Master to tell me what I knew before. What I want to know is *how*?'

'Go and find out,' said the Devil.

We turned to the door, and I was aware that my Characters had grouped themselves at the exit. 'They are going to give you an ovation. Think o' that, now!' said the Devil. I shuddered and dropped my eyes, while one-and-fifty voices broke into a wailing song, whereof the words, so far as I recollect, ran:–

> But we, brought forth and reared in hours
>   Of change, alarm, surprise,
> What shelter to grow ripe is ours –
>   What leisure to grow wise?

I ran the gauntlet, narrowly missed collision with an impetuous soul (I hoped he liked his Characters when he met them), and flung free into the night, where I should have knocked my head against the stars. But the Devil caught me.

*   *   *   *   *

THE brain-fever bird was fluting across the grey, dewy lawn, and the punkah had stopped again. 'Go to Jehannum and get another man to pull,' I said drowsily.

'Exactly,' said a voice from the inkpot.

Now the proof that this story is absolutely true lies in the fact that there will be no other to follow it.

L'ENVOI

My new-cut ashlar takes the light
   Where crimson-blank the windows flare;
By my own work, before the night,
   Great Overseer I make my prayer.

If there be good in that I wrought,
   Thy hand compelled it, Master, Thine;
Where I have failed to meet Thy thought
   I know, through Thee, the blame is mine.

One instant's toil to Thee denied
   Stands all Eternity's offence,
Of that I did with Thee to guide
   To Thee, through Thee, be excellence.

Who, lest all thought of Eden fade,
   Bring'st Eden to the craftsman's brain,
Godlike to muse o'er his own trade
   And Manlike stand with God again.

The depth and dream of my desire,
   The bitter paths wherein I stray,
Thou knowest Who hast made the Fire,
   Thou knowest Who hast made the Clay.

One stone the more swings to her place
   In that dread Temple of Thy Worth –
It is enough that through Thy grace
   I saw naught common on Thy earth.

Take not that vision from my ken;
   Oh whatsoe'er may spoil or speed,
Help me to need no aid from men
   That I may help such men as need!

'THE FINEST STORY IN THE WORLD'

Or ever the knightly years were gone
    With the old world to the grave,
I was a king in Babylon
    And you were a Christian slave.

W. E. Henley

HIS name was Charlie Mears; he was the only son of his mother who was a widow, and he lived in the north of London, coming into the City every day to work in a bank. He was twenty years old and was full of aspirations. I met him in a public billiard-saloon where the marker called him by his first name, and he called the marker 'Bullseye'. Charlie explained, a little nervously, that he had only come to the place to look on, and since looking on at games of skill is not a cheap amusement for the young, I suggested that Charlie should go back to his mother.

That was our first step towards better acquaintance. He would call on me sometimes in the evenings instead of running about London with his fellow-clerks; and before long, speaking of himself as a young man must, he told me of his aspirations, which were all literary. He desired to make himself an undying name chiefly through verse, though he was not above sending stories of love and death to the penny-in-the-slot journals. It was my fate to sit still while Charlie read me poems of many hundred lines, and bulky fragments of plays that would surely shake the world. My reward was his unreserved confidence, and the self-revelations and troubles of a young man are almost as holy as those of a maiden. Charlie had never fallen in love, but was anxious to do so on the first opportunity; he believed in all things good and all things honourable, but at the same time, was curiously careful to let me see that he knew his way about the world as befitted a bank-clerk on twenty-five shillings a week. He rhymed 'dove' with 'love' and 'moon' with 'June', and devoutly believed that they had never so been rhymed before. The long lame gaps in his plays he filled up with hasty words of apology and description and swept on, seeing all that he intended to do so clearly that he esteemed it already done, and turned to me for applause.

I fancy that his mother did not encourage his aspirations; and I know that his writing-table at home was the edge of his washstand. This he told me almost at the outset of our acquaintance – when he was ravaging my bookshelves, and a little before I was implored to speak the truth as to his chances of 'writing something really great, you know'. Maybe I encouraged him too much, for, one night, he called on me, his eyes flaming with excitement, and said breathlessly:–

'Do you mind – can you let me stay here and write all this evening? I won't interrupt you, I won't really. There's no place for me to write in at my mother's.'

'What's the trouble?' I said, knowing well what that trouble was.

'I've a notion in my head that would make the most splendid story that was ever written. Do let me write it out here. It's *such* a notion!'

There was no resisting the appeal. I set him a table; he hardly thanked me, but plunged into his work at once. For half an hour the pen scratched without stopping. Then Charlie sighed and tugged his hair. The scratching grew slower, there were more erasures, and at last ceased. The finest story in the world would not come forth.

'It looks such awful rot now,' he said mournfully. 'And yet it seemed so good when I was thinking about it. What's wrong?'

I could not dishearten him by saying the truth. So I answered: 'Perhaps you don't feel in the mood for writing.'

'Yes I do – except when I look at this stuff. Ugh!'

'Read me what you've done,' I said.

He read, and it was wondrous bad, and he paused at all the specially turgid sentences, expecting a little approval;

for he was proud of those sentences, as I knew he would be.

'It needs compression,' I suggested cautiously.

'I hate cutting my things down. I don't think you could alter a word here without spoiling the sense. It reads better aloud than when I was writing it.'

'Charlie, you're suffering from an alarming disease afflicting a numerous class. Put the thing by, and tackle it again in a week.'

'I want to do it at once. What do you think of it?'

'How can I judge from a half-written tale? Tell me the story as it lies in your head.'

Charlie told, and in the telling there was everything that his ignorance had so carefully prevented from escaping into the written word. I looked at him, wondering whether it were possible that he did not know the originality, the power of the notion that had come in his way? It was distinctly a Notion among notions. Men had been puffed up with pride by ideas not a tithe as excellent and practicable. But Charlie babbled on serenely, interrupting the current of pure fancy with samples of horrible sentences that he purposed to use. I heard him out to the end. It would be folly to allow his thought to remain in his own inept hands, when I could do so much with it. Not all that could be done indeed; but, oh so much!

'What do you think?' he said at last. 'I fancy I shall call it "The Story of a Ship".'

'I think the idea's pretty good; but you won't be able to handle it for ever so long. Now I – '

'Would it be of any use to you? Would you care to take it? I should be proud,' said Charlie promptly.

There are few things sweeter in this world than the guileless, hot-headed, intemperate, open admiration of a junior. Even a woman in her blindest devotion does not fall into the gait of the man she adores, tilt her bonnet to the angle at which he wears his hat, or interlard her speech with his pet oaths. And Charlie did all these things. Still it was necessary to salve my conscience before I possessed myself of Charlie's thoughts.

'Let's make a bargain. I'll give you a fiver for the notion,' I said.

Charlie became a bank-clerk at once.

'Oh, that's impossible. Between two pals, you know, if I may call you so, and speaking as a man of the world, I couldn't. Take the notion if it's any use to you. I've heaps more.'

He had – none knew this better than I – but they were the notions of other men.

'Look at it as a matter of business – between men of the world,' I returned. 'Five pounds will buy you any number of poetry-books. Business is business, and you may be sure I shouldn't give that price unless – '

'Oh, if you put it *that* way,' said Charlie, visibly moved by the thought of the books. The bargain was clinched with an agreement that he should at unstated intervals come to me with all the notions that he possessed, should have a table of his own to write at, an unquestioned right to inflict upon me all his poems and fragments of poems. Then I said, 'Now tell me how you came by this idea.'

'It came by itself.' Charlie's eyes opened a little.

'Yes, but you told me a great deal about the hero that you must have read before somewhere.'

'I haven't any time for reading, except when you let me sit here, and on Sundays I'm on my bicycle or down the river all day. There's nothing wrong about the hero, is there?'

'Tell me again and I shall understand clearly. You say that your hero went pirating. How did he live?'

'He was on the lower deck of this ship-thing that I was telling you about.'

'What sort of ship?'

'It was the kind rowed with oars, and the sea spurts through the oar-holes and the men row sitting up to their knees in water. Then there's a bench running down between the two lines of oars and an overseer with a whip walks up and down the bench to make the men work.'

'How do you know that?'

'It's in the tale. There's a rope running overhead, looped to the upper deck, for the overseer to catch hold of when the ship rolls. When the overseer misses the rope once and falls among the rowers, remember the hero laughs at him and gets licked for it. He's chained to his oar of course – the hero.'

'How is he chained?'

'With an iron band round his waist, fixed to the bench he sits on, and a sort of handcuff on his left wrist chaining him to the oar. He's on the lower deck where the worst men are sent, and the only light comes from the hatchways and through the oar-holes. Can't you imagine the sunlight just squeezing through between the handle and the hole and wobbling about as the ship moves?'

'I can, but I can't imagine your imagining it.'

'How could it be any other way? Now you listen to me. The long oars on the upper deck are managed by four men to each bench, the lower ones by three, and the lowest of all by two. Remember it's quite dark on the lowest deck and all the men there go mad. When a man dies at his oar on that deck he isn't thrown overboard, but cut up in his chains and stuffed through the oar-hole in little pieces.'

'Why?' I demanded amazed, not so much at the information as the tone of command in which it was flung out.

'To save trouble and to frighten the others. It needs two overseers to drag a man's body up to the top deck; and if the men at the lower deck oars were left alone, of course they'd stop rowing and try to pull up the benches by all standing up together in their chains.'

'You've a most provident imagination. Where have you been reading about galleys and galley-slaves?'

'Nowhere that I remember. I row a little when I get the chance. But, perhaps, if you say so, I may have read something.'

He went away shortly afterwards to deal with booksellers, and I wondered how a bank-clerk aged twenty could put into my hands with a profligate abundance of detail, all given with absolute assurance, the story of extravagant and bloodthirsty adventure, riot, piracy, and death in unnamed seas. He had led his hero a desperate dance through revolt against the overseers, to command of a ship of his own, and at last to the establishment of a kingdom on an island 'somewhere in the sea, you know'; and, delighted with my paltry five pounds, had gone out to buy the notions of other men, that these might teach him how to write. I had the consolation of knowing that this notion was mine by right of purchase, and I thought that I could make something of it.

When next he came to me he was drunk´– royally drunk on many poets for the first time revealed to him. His pupils were dilated, his words tumbled over each other, and he wrapped himself in quotations – as a beggar would enfold himself in the purple of Emperors. Most of all was he drunk with Longfellow.

'Isn't it splendid? Isn't it superb?' he cried, after hasty greetings. 'Listen to this –

> 'Wouldst thou,' – so the helmsman answered,
>   'Know the secret of the sea?
> Only those who brave its dangers
>   Comprehend its mystery.'

By gum!

> 'Only those who brave its dangers
>   Comprehend its mystery,'

he repeated twenty times, walking up and down the room and forgetting me. 'But *I* can understand it too,' he said to himself. 'I don't know how to thank you for that fiver. And this; listen –

> I remember the black wharves and the slips
>   And the sea-tides tossing free;
> And the Spanish sailors with bearded lips,
> And the beauty and mystery of the ships,
>   And the magic of the sea.

I haven't braved any dangers, but I feel as if I knew all about it.'

'You certainly seem to have a grip of the sea. Have you ever seen it?'

'When I was a little chap I went to Brighton once; we used

to live in Coventry, though, before we came to London. I never saw it,

> When descends on the Atlantic
> The gigantic
> Storm-wind of the Equinox.

He shook me by the shoulder to make me understand the passion that was shaking himself.

'When that storm comes,' he continued, 'I think that all the oars in the ship that I was talking about get broken, and the rowers have their chests smashed in by the oar-heads bucking. By the way, have you done anything with that notion of mine yet?'

'No. I was waiting to hear more of it from you. Tell me how in the world you're so certain about the fittings of the ship. You know nothing of ships.'

'I don't know. It's as real as anything to me until I try to write it down. I was thinking about it only last night in bed, after you had lent me *Treasure Island*; and I made up a whole lot of new things to go into the story.'

'What sort of things?'

'About the food the men ate; rotten figs and black beans and wine in a skin bag, passed from bench to bench.'

'Was the ship built so long ago as *that*?'

'As what? I don't know whether it was long ago or not. It's only a notion, but sometimes it seems just as real as if it was true. Do I bother you with talking about it?'

'Not in the least. Did you make up anything else?'

'Yes, but it's nonsense.' Charlie flushed a little.

'Never mind; let's hear about it.'

'Well, I was thinking over the story, and after awhile I got out of bed and wrote down on a piece of paper the sort of stuff the men might be supposed to scratch on their oars with the edges of their handcuffs. It seemed to make the thing more life-like. It *is* so real to me, y'know.'

'Have you the paper on you?'

'Ye – es, but what's the use of showing it? It's only a lot of scratches. All the same, we might have 'em reproduced in the book on the front page.'

'I'll attend to those details. Show me what your men wrote.'

He pulled out of his pocket a sheet of notepaper, with a single line of scratches upon it, and I put this carefully away.

'What is it supposed to mean in English?' I said.

'Oh, I don't know. I mean it to mean "I'm beastly tired." It's great nonsense,' he repeated, 'but all those men in the ship seem as real as real people to me. Do do something to the notion soon; I should like to see it written and printed.'

'But all you've told me would make a long book.'

'Make it then. You've only to sit down and write it out.'

'Give me a little time. Have you any more notions?'

'Not just now. I'm reading all the books I've bought. They're splendid.'

When he had left I looked at the sheet of notepaper with the inscription upon it. Then I took my head tenderly between both hands, to make certain that it was not coming off or turning round. Then . . . but there seemed to be no interval between quitting my rooms and finding myself arguing with a policeman outside a door marked *Private* in a corridor of the British Museum. All I demanded, as politely as possible, was 'the Greek antiquity man'. The policeman knew nothing except the rules of the Museum, and it became necessary to forage through all the houses and offices inside the gates. An elderly gentleman called away from his lunch put an end to my search by holding the notepaper between finger and thumb and sniffing at it scornfully.

'What does this mean? H'mm,' said he. 'So far as I can ascertain it is an attempt to write extremely corrupt Greek on the part' – here he glared at me with intention – 'of an extremely illiterate – ah – person.' He read slowly from the paper, '*Pollock, Erckmann, Tauchnitz, Henniker*' – four names familiar to me.

'Can you tell me what the corruption is supposed to mean – the gist of the thing?' I asked.

'I have been – many times – overcome with weariness in this particular employment. That is the meaning.' He returned me the paper, and I fled without a word of thanks, explanation, or apology.

I might have been excused for forgetting much. To me of all men had been given the chance to write the most marvellous tale in the world, nothing less than the story of a Greek galley-slave, as told by himself. Small wonder that his dreaming had seemed real to Charlie. The Fates that are so careful to shut the doors of each successive life behind us had, in this case, been neglectful, and Charlie was looking, though that he did not know, where never man had been permitted to look with full knowledge since Time began. Above all, he was absolutely ignorant of the knowledge sold to me for five pounds; and he would retain that ignorance, for bank-clerks do not understand metempsychosis, and a sound commercial education does not include Greek. He would supply me – here I capered among the dumb gods of Egypt and laughed in their battered faces – with material to make my tale sure – so sure that the world would hail it as an impudent and vamped fiction. And I – I alone would know that it was absolutely and literally true. I – I alone held this jewel to my hand for the cutting and polishing! Therefore I danced again among the gods of the Egyptian court till a policeman saw me and took steps in my direction.

It remained now only to encourage Charlie to talk, and here there was no difficulty. But I had forgotten those accursed books of poetry. He came to me time after time, as useless as a surcharged phonograph – drunk on Byron, Shelley, or Keats. Knowing now what the boy had been in his past lives, and desperately anxious not to lose one word of his babble, I could not hide from him any respect and interest. He misconstrued both into respect for the present soul of Charlie Mears, to whom life was as new as it was to Adam, and interest in his readings; and stretched my patience to breaking point by reciting poetry – not his own now, but that of others. I wished every English poet blotted out of the memory of mankind. I blasphemed the mightiest names of song because they had drawn Charlie from the path of direct narrative, and would, later, spur him to imitate them; but I choked down my impatience until the first flood of enthusiasm should have spent itself and the boy returned to his dreams.

'What's the use of my telling you what *I* think, when these chaps wrote things for the angels to read?' he growled, one evening. 'Why don't you write something like theirs?'

'I don't think you're treating me quite fairly,' I said, speaking under strong restraint.

'I've given you the story,' he said shortly, replunging into 'Lara'.

'But I want the details.'

'The things I make up about that damned ship that you call a galley? They're quite easy. You can just make 'em up for yourself. Turn up the gas a little, I want to go on reading.'

I could have broken the gas globe over his head for his amazing stupidity. I could indeed make up things for myself did I only know what Charlie did not know that he knew. But since the doors were shut behind me I could only wait his youthful pleasure and strive to keep him in good temper. One minute's want of guard might spoil a priceless revelation: now and again he would toss his books aside – he kept them in my rooms, for his mother would have been shocked at the waste of good money had she seen them – and launched into his sea-dreams. Again I cursed all the poets of England. The plastic mind of the bank-clerk had been overlaid, coloured, and distorted by that which he had read, and the result as delivered was a confused tangle of other voices most like the mutter and hum through a City telephone in the busiest part of the day.

He talked of the galley – his own galley had he but known it – with illustrations borrowed from the 'Bride of Abydos'. He pointed the experiences of his hero with quotations from 'The Corsair', and threw in deep and desperate moral reflections from 'Cain' and 'Manfred', expecting me to use them all. Only when the talk turned on Longfellow were the jarring cross-currents dumb, and I knew that Charlie was speaking the truth as he remembered it.

'What do you think of this?' I said one evening, as soon as I understood the medium in which his memory worked best, and, before he could expostulate, read him nearly the whole of 'The Saga of King Olaf'!

He listened open-mouthed, flushed, his hands drumming on the back of the sofa where he lay, till I came to the Song of Einar Tamberskelver and the verse:–

> Einar then, the arrow taking
> From the loosened string,
> Answered, 'That was Norway breaking
> 'Neath thy hand, O King.'

He gasped with pure delight of sound.

'That's better than Byron, a little?' I ventured.

'Better! Why it's *true*! How could he have known?'

I went back and repeated:–

> 'What was that?' said Olaf, standing
> On the quarter-deck,
> 'Something heard I like the stranding
> Of a shattered wreck.'

'How could he have known how the ships crash and the oars rip out and go *z-zzp* all along the line? Why only the other night . . . But go back please and read "The Skerry of Shrieks" again.'

'No, I'm tired. Let's talk. What happened the other night?'

'I had an awful dream about that galley of ours. I dreamed I was drowned in a fight. You see we ran alongside another ship in harbour. The water was dead still except where our oars whipped it up. You know where I always sit in the galley?' He spoke haltingly at first, under a fine English fear of being laughed at.

'No. That's news to me,' I answered meekly, my heart beginning to beat.

'On the fourth oar from the bow on the right side of the upper deck. There were four of us at that oar, all chained. I remember watching the water and trying to get my handcuffs off before the row began. Then we closed up on the other ship, and all their fighting men jumped over our bulwarks, and my bench broke and I was pinned down with the three other fellows on top of me, and the big oar jammed across our backs.'

'Well?' Charlie's eyes were alive and alight. He was looking at the wall behind my chair.

'I don't know how we fought. The men were trampling all over my back, and I lay low. Then our rowers on the left side – tied to their oars, you know – began to yell and back water. I could hear the water sizzle, and we spun round like a cockchafer and I knew, lying where I was, that there was a galley coming up bow-on, to ram us on the left side. I could just lift my head and see her sail over the bulwarks. We wanted to meet her bow to bow, but it was too late. We could only turn a little bit because the galley on our right had hooked herself on to us and stopped our moving. Then, by gum! There was a crash! Our left oars began to break as the other galley, the moving one y'know, stuck her nose into them. Then the lower-deck oars shot up through the deck planking, butt first, and one of them jumped clear up into the air and came down again close at my head.'

'How was that managed?'

'The moving galley's bow was plunking them back through their own oar-holes, and I could hear no end of a shindy in the decks below. Then her nose caught us nearly in the middle, and we tilted sideways, and the fellows in the right-hand galley unhitched their hooks and ropes, and threw things on to our upper deck – arrows, and hot pitch or something that stung, and we went up and up and up on the left side, and the right side dipped, and I twisted my head round and saw the water stand still as it topped the right bulwarks, and then it curled over and crashed down on the whole lot of us on the right side, and I felt it hit my back, and I woke.'

'One minute, Charlie. When the sea topped the bulwarks, what did it look like?' I had my reasons for asking. A man of my acquaintance had once gone down with a leaking ship in a still sea, and had seen the water-level pause for an instant ere it fell on the deck.

'It looked just like a banjo-string drawn tight, and it seemed to stay there for years,' said Charlie.

Exactly! The other man had said: 'It looked like a silver wire laid down along the bulwarks, and I thought it was never going to break.' He had paid everything except the bare life for this little valueless piece of knowledge, and I had travelled ten thousand weary miles to meet him and take his knowledge at second hand. But Charlie, the bank-clerk on twenty-five shillings a week, who had never been out of sight of a made road, knew it all. It was no consolation to me that once in his lives he had been forced to die for his gains. I also must have died scores of times, but behind me, because I could have used my knowledge, the doors were shut.

'And then?' I said, trying to put away the devil of envy.

'The funny thing was, though, in all the row I didn't feel a bit astonished or frightened. It seemed as if I'd been in a good many fights, because I told my next man so when the row began. But that cad of an overseer on my deck wouldn't unloose our chains and give us a chance. He always said that we'd all be set free after a battle, but we never were; we never were.' Charlie shook his head mournfully.

'What a scoundrel!'

'I should say he was. He never gave us enough to eat, and sometimes we were so thirsty that we used to drink salt-water. I can taste that salt-water still.'

'Now tell me something about the harbour where the fight was fought.'

'I didn't dream about that. I know it was a harbour, though; because we were tied up to a ring on a white wall and all the face of the stone under water was covered with wood to prevent our ram getting chipped when the tide made us rock.'

'That's curious. Our hero commanded the galley, didn't he?'

'Didn't he just! He stood by the bows and shouted like a good 'un. He was the man who killed the overseer.'

'But you were all drowned together, Charlie, weren't you?'

'I can't make that fit quite,' he said, with a puzzled look. 'The galley must have gone down with all hands, and yet

I fancy that the hero went on living afterwards. Perhaps he climbed into the attacking ship. I wouldn't see that, of course. I was dead, you know.'

He shivered slightly and protested that he could remember no more.

I did not press him further, but to satisfy myself that he lay in ignorance of the workings of his own mind, deliberately introduced him to Mortimer Collins's *Transmigration*, and gave him a sketch of the plot before he opened the pages.

'What rot it all is!' he said frankly, at the end of an hour. 'I don't understand his nonsense about the Red Planet Mars and the King, and the rest of it. Chuck me the Longfellow again.'

I handed him the book and wrote out as much as I could remember of his description of the sea-fight, appealing to him from time to time for confirmation of fact or detail. He would answer without raising his eyes from the book, as assuredly as though all his knowledge lay before him on the printed page. I spoke under the normal key of my voice that the current might not be broken, and I knew that he was not aware of what he was saying, for his thoughts were out on the sea with Longfellow.

'Charlie,' I asked, 'when the rowers on the galleys mutinied how did they kill their overseers?'

'Tore up the benches and brained 'em. That happened when a heavy sea was running. An overseer on the lower deck slipped from the centre plank and fell among the rowers. They choked him to death against the side of the ship with their chained hands quite quietly, and it was too dark for the other overseer to see what had happened. When he asked, he was pulled down too and choked, and the lower deck fought their way up deck by deck, with the pieces of the broken benches banging behind 'em. How they howled!'

'And what happened after that?'

'I don't know. The hero went away – red hair and red beard and all. That was after he had captured our galley, I think.'

The sound of my voice irritated him, and he motioned slightly with his left hand as a man does when interruption jars.

'You never told me he was red-headed before, or that he captured your galley,' I said, after a discreet interval.

Charlie did not raise his eyes.

'He was as red as a red bear,' said he abstractedly. 'He came from the north; they said so in the galley when he looked for rowers – not slaves, but free men. Afterwards – years and years afterwards – news came from another ship, or else he came back –'

His lips moved in silence. He was rapturously retasting some poem before him.

'Where had he been, then?' I was almost whispering that the sentence might come gently to whichever section of Charlie's brain was working on my behalf.

'To the Beaches – the Long and Wonderful Beaches!' was the reply after a minute of silence.

'To Furdurstrandi?' I asked, tingling from head to foot.

'Yes, to Furdurstrandi,' he pronounced the word in a new fashion. 'And I too saw – ' The voice failed.

'Do you know what you have said?' I shouted incautiously.

He lifted his eyes, fully roused now. 'No!' he snapped. 'I wish you'd let a chap go on reading. Hark to this:–

> But Othere, the old sea captain,
> He neither paused nor stirred
>   Till the king listened, and then
>   Once more took up his pen
> And wrote down every word.
>
>
> And to the King of the Saxons
> In witness of the truth,
>   Raising his noble head,
>   He stretched his brown hand and said,
> 'Behold this walrus tooth.'

By Jove, what chaps those must have been, to go sailing all over the shop never knowing where they'd fetch the land! Hah!'

'Charlie,' I pleaded, 'if you'll only be sensible for a minute or two I'll make our hero in our tale every inch as good as Othere.'

'Umph! Longfellow wrote that poem. I don't care about writing things any more. I want to read.' He was thoroughly out of tune now, and raging over my own ill-luck, I left him.

Conceive yourself at the door of the world's treasure-house guarded by a child – an idle irresponsible child playing knuckle-bones – on whose favour depends the gift of the key, and you will imagine one-half my torment. Till that evening Charlie had spoken nothing that might not lie within the experiences of a Greek galley-slave. But now, or there was no virtue in books, he had talked of some desperate adventure of the Vikings, of Thorfin Karlsefne's sailing to Wineland, which is America, in the ninth or tenth century. The battle in the harbour he had seen; and his own death he had described. But this was a much more startling plunge into the past. Was it possible that he had skipped half a dozen lives and was then dimly remembering some episode of a thousand years later? It was a maddening jumble, and the worst of it was that Charlie Mears in his normal condition was the last person in the world to clear it up. I could only wait and watch, but I went to bed that night full of the wildest imaginings. There was nothing that was not possible if Charlie's detestable memory only held good.

I might rewrite the Saga of Thorfin Karlsefne as it had never been written before, might tell the story of the first discovery of America, myself the discoverer. But I was entirely at Charlie's mercy, and so long as there was a three-and-sixpenny Bohn volume within his reach Charlie would not tell. I dared not curse him openly; I hardly dared jog his memory, for I was dealing with the experiences of a thousand years ago, told through the mouth of a boy of to-day; and a boy of to-day is affected by every change of tone and gust of opinion, so that he must lie even when he most desires to speak the truth.

I saw no more of Charlie for nearly a week. When next I met him it was in Gracechurch Street with a bill-book chained to his waist. Business took him over London Bridge, and I accompanied him. He was very full of the importance of that book and magnified it. As we passed over the Thames we paused to look at a steamer unloading great slabs of white and brown marble. A barge drifted under the steamer's stern and a lonely ship's cow in that barge bellowed. Charlie's face changed from the face of the bank-clerk to that of an unknown and – though he would not have believed this – a much shrewder man. He flung out his arm across the parapet of the bridge and laughing very loudly, said:–

'When they heard *our* bulls bellow the Skroelings ran away!'

I waited only for an instant, but the barge and the cow had disappeared under the bows of the steamer before I answered.

'Charlie, what do you suppose are Skroelings?'

'Never heard of 'em before. They sound like a new kind of sea-gull. What a chap you are for asking questions!' he replied. 'I have to go to the cashier of the Omnibus Company yonder. Will you wait for me and we can lunch somewhere together? I've a notion for a poem.'

'No, thanks. I'm off. You're sure you know nothing about Skroelings?'

'Not unless he's been entered for the Liverpool Handicap.' He nodded and disappeared in the crowd.

Now it is written in the Saga of Eric the Red or that of Thorfin Karlsefne, that nine hundred years ago when Karlsefne's galleys came to Leif's booths, which Leif had erected in the unknown land called Markland, which may or may not have been Rhode Island, the Skroelings – and the Lord He knows who these may or may not have been – came to trade with the Vikings, and ran away because they were frightened at the bellowing of the cattle which Thorfin had brought with him in the ships. But what in the world could a Greek slave know of that affair? I wandered up and down among the streets trying to unravel the mystery, and the more I considered it, the more baffling it grew. One thing only seemed certain, and that certainty took away my breath for the moment. If I came to full knowledge of anything at all, it would not be one life of the soul in Charlie Mears's body, but half a dozen – half a dozen several and separate existences spent on blue water in the morning of the world!

Then I reviewed the situation.

Obviously if I used my knowledge I should stand alone

and unapproachable until all men were as wise as myself. That would be something, but manlike I was ungrateful. It seemed bitterly unfair that Charlie's memory should fail me when I needed it most. Great Powers Above – I looked up at them through the fog-smoke – did the Lords of Life and Death know what this meant to me? Nothing less than eternal fame of the best kind, that comes from One, and is shared by one alone. I would be content – remembering Clive, I stood astounded at my own moderation – with the mere right to tell one story, to work out one little contribution to the light literature of the day. If Charlie were permitted full recollection for one hour – for sixty short minutes – of existences that had extended over a thousand years – I would forego all profit and honour from all that I should make of his speech. I would take no share in the commotion that would follow throughout the particular corner of the earth that calls itself 'the world'. The thing should be put forth anonymously. Nay, I would make other men believe that they had written it. They would hire bull-hided self-advertising Englishmen to bellow it abroad. Preachers would found a fresh conduct of life upon it, swearing that it was new and that they had lifted the fear of death from all mankind. Every Orientalist in Europe would patronise it discursively with Sanskrit and Pali texts. Terrible women would invent unclean variants of the men's belief for the elevation of their sisters. Churches and religions would war over it. Between the hailing and re-starting of an omnibus I foresaw the scuffles that would arise among half a dozen denominations all professing 'the doctrine of the True Metempsychosis as applied to the world and the New Era'; and saw, too, the respectable English newspapers shying, like frightened kine, over the beautiful simplicity of the tale. The mind leaped forward a hundred – two hundred – a thousand years. I saw with sorrow that men would mutilate and garble the story; that rival creeds would turn it upside down till, at last, the western world which clings to the dread of death more closely than the hope of life, would set it aside as an interesting superstition and stampede after some faith so long forgotten that it seemed altogether new. Upon this I changed the terms of the bargain that I would make with the Lords of Life and Death. Only let me know, let me write, the story with sure knowledge that I wrote the truth, and I would burn the manuscript as a solemn sacrifice. Five minutes after the last line was written I would destroy it all. But I must be allowed to write it with absolute certainty.

There was no answer. The flaming colours of an Aquarium poster caught my eye, and I wondered whether it would be wise or prudent to lure Charlie into the hands of the professional mesmerist then, and whether, if he were under his power, he would speak of his past lives. If he did, and if people believed him . . . but Charlie would be frightened and flustered, or made conceited by the interviews. In either case he would begin to lie, through fear or vanity. He was safest in my own hands.

'They are very funny fools, your English,' said a voice at my elbow, and turning round I recognised a casual acquaintance, a young Bengali law student, called Grish Chunder, whose father had sent him to England to become civilised. The old man was a retired native official, and on an income of five pounds a month contrived to allow his son two hundred pounds a year, and the run of his teeth in a city where he could pretend to be the cadet of a royal house, and tell stories of the brutal Indian bureaucrats who ground the faces of the poor.

Grish Chunder was a young, fat, full-bodied Bengali, dressed with scrupulous care in frock coat, tall hat, light trousers, and tan gloves. But I had known him in the days when the brutal Indian Government paid for his university education, and he contributed cheap sedition to the *Sachi Durpan*, and intrigued with the wives of his fourteen-year-old schoolmates.

'That is very funny and very foolish,' he said, nodding at the poster. 'I am going down to the Northbrook Club. Will you come too?'

I walked with him for some time. 'You are not well,' he said. 'What is there on your mind? You do not talk.'

'Grish Chunder, you've been too well educated to believe in a God, haven't you?'

'Oah, yes, *here*! But when I go home I must conciliate popular superstition, and make ceremonies of purification, and my women will anoint idols.'

'And hang up *tulsi* and feast the *purohit*, and take you back into caste again and make a good *khuttri* of you again, you advanced Freethinker. And you'll eat *desi* food, and like it all, from the smell in the courtyard to the mustard oil over you.'

'I shall very much like it,' said Grish Chunder unguardedly. 'Once a Hindu – always a Hindu. But I like to know what the English think they know.'

'I'll tell you something that one Englishman knows. It's an old tale to you.'

I began to tell the story of Charlie in English, but Grish Chunder put a question in the vernacular, and the history went forward naturally in the tongue best suited for its telling. After all, it could never have been told in English. Grish Chunder heard me, nodding from time to time, and then came up to my rooms, where I finished the tale.

'*Beshak*,' he said philosophically. '*Lekin darwaza band hai.* (Without doubt; but the door is shut.) I have heard of this remembering of previous existences among my people. It is of course an old tale with us, but, to happen to an Englishman – a cow-fed *Mlechh* – an outcast. By Jove, that is *most* peculiar!'

'Outcast yourself, Grish Chunder! You eat cow-beef every day. Let's think the thing over. The boy remembers his incarnations.'

'Does he know that?' said Grish Chunder quietly, swinging his legs as he sat on my table. He was speaking in his English now.

'He does not know anything. Would I speak to you if he did? Go on !'

'There is no going on at all. If you tell that to your friends they will say you are mad and put it in the papers. Suppose, now, you prosecute for libel.'

'Let's leave that out of the question entirely. Is there any chance of his being made to speak?'

'There is a chance. Oah, yess! But *if* he spoke it would mean that all this world would end now – *instanto* – fall down on your head. These things are not allowed, you know. As I said, the door is shut.'

'Not a ghost of a chance?'

'How can there be? You are a Christi-án, and it is forbidden to eat, in your books, of the Tree of Life, or else you would never die. How shall you all fear death if you all know what your friend does not know that he knows? I am afraid to be kicked, but I am not afraid to die, because I know what I know. You are not afraid to be kicked, but you are afraid to die. If you were not, by God! you English would be all over the shop in an hour, upsetting the balances of power, and making commotions. It would not be good. But no fear. He will remember a little and a little less, and he will call it dreams. Then he will forget altogether. When I passed my First Arts Examination in Calcutta that was all in the crambook on Wordsworth. "Trailing clouds of glory," you know.'

'This seems to be an exception to the rule.'

'There are no exceptions to rules. Some are not so hard-looking as others, but they are all the same when you touch. If this friend of yours said so-and-so and so-and-so, indicating that he remembered all his lost lives, or one piece of a lost life, he would not be in the bank another hour. He would be what you called sack because he was mad, and they would send him to an asylum for lunatics. You can see that, my friend.'

'Of course I can, but I wasn't thinking of him. His name need never appear in the story,'

'Ah! I see. That story will never be written. You can try.'

'I am going to.'

'For your own credit and for the sake of money, *of* course?'

'No. For the sake of writing the story. On my honour that will be all.'

'Even then there is no chance. You cannot play with the

gods. It is a very pretty story now. As they say, Let it go on that – I mean at that. Be quick; he will not last long.'

'How do you mean?'

'What I say. He has never, so far, thought about a woman.'

'Hasn't he, though!' I remembered some of Charlie's confidences.

'I mean no woman has thought about him. When that comes; *bus – hogya* – all up! I know. There are millions of women here. Housemaids, for instance. They kiss you behind doors.'

I winced at the thought of my story being ruined by a housemaid. And yet nothing was more probable.

Grish Chunder grinned.

'Yes – also pretty girls – cousins of his house, and perhaps *not* of his house. One kiss that he gives back again and remembers will cure all this nonsense, or else – '

'Or else what? Remember he does not know that he knows.'

'I know that. Or else, if nothing happens he will become immersed in the trade and the financial speculation like the rest. It must be so. You can see that it must be so. But the woman will come first, *I* think.'

There was a rap at the door, and Charlie charged in impetuously. He had been released from office, and by the look in his eyes I could see that he had come over for a long talk; most probably with poems in his pockets. Charlie's poems were very wearying, but sometimes they led him to speak about the galley.

Grish Chunder looked at him keenly for a minute.

'I beg your pardon,' Charlie said uneasily; 'I didn't know you had any one with you.'

'I am going,' said Grish Chunder.

He drew me into the lobby as he departed.

'That is your man,' he said quickly. 'I tell you he will never speak all you wish. That is rot – bosh. But he would be most good to make to see things. Suppose now we pretend that it was only play' – I had never seen Grish Chunder so excited – 'and pour the ink-pool into his hand. Eh, what do you think? I tell you that he could see *anything* that a man could see. Let

me get the ink and the camphor. He is a seer and he will tell
us very many things.'

'He may be all you say, but I'm not going to trust him to
your gods and devils.'

'It will not hurt him. He will only feel a little stupid and dull
when he wakes up. You have seen boys look into the ink-pool
before.'

'That is the reason why I am not going to see it any more.
You'd better go, Grish Chunder.'

He went, insisting far down the staircase that it was throwing
away my only chance of looking into the future.

This left me unmoved, for I was concerned for the past, and
no peering of hypnotised boys into mirrors and ink-pools would
help me to that. But I recognised Grish Chunder's point of
view and sympathised with it.

'What a big black brute that was!' said Charlie, when I
returned to him. 'Well, look here, I've just done a poem; did
it instead of playing dominoes after lunch. May I read it?'

'Let me read it to myself.'

'Then you miss the proper expression. Besides, you always
make my things sound as if the rhymes were all wrong.'

'Read it aloud, then. You're like the rest of 'em.'

Charlie mouthed me his poem, and it was not much worse
than the average of his verses. He had been reading his books
faithfully, but he was not pleased when I told him that I
preferred my Longfellow undiluted with Charlie.

Then we began to go through the MS. line by line; Charlie
parrying every objection and correction with:

'Yes, that may be better, but you don't catch what I'm
driving at.'

Charlie was, in one way at least, very like one kind of
poet.

There was a pencil scrawl at the back of the paper and
'What's that?' I said.

'Oh that's not poetry at all. It's some rot I wrote last
night before I went to bed, and it was too much bother
to hunt for rhymes; so I made it a sort of blank verse
instead.

Here is Charlie's 'blank verse':–

We pulled for you when the wind was against us and the sails were low.
Will you never let us go?
We ate bread and onions when you took towns, or ran aboard quickly when you were beaten back by the foe,
The captains walked up and down the deck in fair weather singing songs, but we were below,
We fainted with our chins on the oars and you did not see that we were idle for we still swung to and fro.
Will you never let us go?
The salt made the oar-handles like shark-skin; our knees were cut to the bone with salt cracks; our hair was stuck to our foreheads; and our lips were cut to our gums and you whipped us because we could not row.
Will you never let us go?
But in a little time we shall run out of the portholes as the water runs along the oar-blade, and though you tell the others to row after us you will never catch us till you catch the oar-thresh and tie up the winds in the belly of the sail. Aho!
Will you never let us go?

'H'm. What's oar-thresh, Charlie?'
'The water washed up by the oars. That's the sort of song they might sing in the galley y'know. Aren't you ever going to finish that story and give me some of the profits?'
'It depends on yourself. If you had only told me more about your hero in the first instance it might have been finished by now. You're so hazy in your notions.'
'I only want to give you the general notion of it – the knocking about from place to place and the fighting and all that. Can't you fill in the rest yourself? Make the hero save a girl on a pirate-galley and marry her or do something.'
'You're a really helpful collaborator. I suppose the hero went through some few adventures before he married.'
'Well then, make him a very artful card – a low sort of man – a sort of political man who went about making treaties and breaking them – a black-haired chap who hid behind the mast when the fighting began.'

'But you said the other day that he was red-haired.'

'I couldn't have. Make him black-haired of course. You've no imagination.'

Seeing that I had just discovered the entire principles upon which the half-memory falsely called imagination is based, I felt entitled to laugh, but forbore, for the sake of the tale.

'You're right. *You're* the man with imagination. A black-haired chap in a decked ship,' I said.

'No, an open ship – like a big boat.'

This was maddening.

'Your ship has been built and designed, closed and decked in; you said so yourself,' I protested.

'No, no, not the ship. That was open or half-decked because – By Jove, you're right. You made me think of the hero as a red-haired chap. Of course if he were red, the ship would be an open one with painted sails.'

Surely, I thought, he would remember now that he had served in two galleys at least – in a three-decked Greek one under the black-haired 'political man', and again in a Viking's open sea-serpent under the man 'red as a red bear' who went to Markland. The devil prompted me to speak.

'Why, ''of course'', Charlie?' said I.

'I don't know. Are you making fun of me?'

The current was broken for the time being. I took up a note-book and pretended to make many entries in it.

'It's a pleasure to work with an imaginative chap like yourself,' I said, after a pause. 'The way that you've brought out the character of the hero is simply wonderful.'

'Do you think so?' he answered, with a pleased flush. 'I often tell myself that there's more in me than my mo – than people think.'

'There's an enormous amount in you.'

'Then, won't you let me send in an essay on The Ways of Bank-Clerks to *Tit-Bits*, and get the guinea prize?'

'That wasn't exactly what I meant, old fellow: perhaps it would be better to wait a little and go ahead with the galley-story.'

'Ah, but I sha'n't get the credit of that. *Tit-Bits* would

publish my name and address if I win. What are you grinning at? They *would*.'

'I know it. Suppose you go for a walk. I want to look through my notes about our story.'

Now this reprehensible youth who left me, a little hurt and put back, might for aught he or I knew have been one of the crew of the Argo – had been certainly slave or comrade to Thorfin Karlsefne. Therefore he was deeply interested in guinea competitions. Remembering what Grish Chunder had said I laughed aloud. The Lords of Life and Death would never allow Charlie Mears to speak with full knowledge of his pasts, and I must even piece out what he had told me with my own poor inventions while Charlie wrote of the ways of bank-clerks.

I got together and placed on one file all my notes; and the net result was not cheering. I read them a second time. There was nothing that might not have been compiled, at second-hand from other people's books – except, perhaps, the story of the fight in the harbour. The adventures of a Viking had been written many times before; the history of a Greek galley-slave was no new thing, and though I wrote both, who could challenge or confirm the accuracy of my details? I might as well tell a tale of two thousand years hence. The Lords of Life and Death were as cunning as Grish Chunder had hinted. They would allow nothing to escape that might trouble or make easy the minds of men. Though I was convinced of this, yet I could not leave the tale alone. Exaltation followed reaction, not once, but twenty times in the next few weeks. My moods varied with the March sunlight and flying clouds. By night or in the beauty of a spring morning I perceived that I could write that tale and shift continents thereby. In the wet windy afternoons, I saw that the tale might indeed be written, but would be nothing more than a faked, false-varnished, sham-rusted piece of Wardour Street work in the end. Then I blessed Charlie in many ways – though it was no fault of his. He seemed to be busy with prize competitions, and I saw less and less of him as the weeks went by and the earth cracked and grew ripe to spring, and the buds swelled in their sheaths. He did not care to read or talk of what he had read, and there was a new ring of self-assertion in his voice. I hardly cared to remind him of the galley when we met; but Charlie alluded to it on every occasion, always as a story from which money was to be made.

'I think I deserve twenty-five per cent, don't I, at least?' he said, with beautiful frankness. 'I supplied all the ideas, didn't I?'

This greediness for silver was a new side in his nature. I assumed that it had been developed in the City, where Charlie was picking up the curious nasal drawl of the underbred City man.

'When the thing's done we'll talk about it. I can't make anything of it at present. Red-haired or black-haired hero are equally difficult.'

He was sitting by the fire staring at the red coals. '*I* can't understand what you find so difficult. It's all as clear as mud to me,' he replied. A jet of gas puffed out between the bars, took light, and whistled softly. 'Suppose we take the red-haired hero's adventures first, from the time that he came south to my galley and captured it and sailed to the Beaches.'

I knew better now than to interrupt Charlie. I was out of reach of pen and paper, and dared not move to get them lest I should break the current. The gas-jet puffed and whinnied, Charlie's voice dropped almost to a whisper, and he told a tale of the sailing of an open galley to Furdurstrandi, of sunsets on the open sea, seen under the curve of the one sail evening after evening when the galley's beak was notched into the centre of the sinking disc, and 'we sailed by that for we had no other guide,' quoth Charlie. He spoke of a landing on an island and explorations in its woods, where the crew killed three men whom they found asleep under the pines. Their ghosts, Charlie said, followed the galley, swimming and choking in the water, and the crew cast lots and threw one of their number overboard as a sacrifice to the strange gods whom they had offended. Then they ate sea-weed when their provisions failed, and their legs swelled, and their leader, the red-haired man, killed two rowers who mutinied, and after a year spent among the woods they set sail for their own country, and a wind that never failed carried them back so safely that they all slept at night. This, and much more Charlie told. Sometimes the voice fell so low that I could not catch the words, though every nerve was on the strain. He spoke of their leader, the red-haired man, as a pagan speaks of his God; for it was he who cheered them and slew them impartially as he thought best for their needs; and it was he who steered them for three days among floating ice, each floe crowded with strange beasts that 'tried to sail with us', said Charlie, 'and we beat them back with the handles of the oars.'

The gas-jet went out, a burnt coal gave way, and the fire settled with a tiny crash to the bottom of the grate. Charlie ceased speaking, and I said no word.

'By Jove!' he said at last, shaking his head. 'I've been staring at the fire till I'm dizzy. What was I going to say?'

'Something about the galley-book.'

'I remember now. It's twenty-five per cent of the profits, isn't it?'

'It's anything you like when I've done the tale.'

'I wanted to be sure of that. I must go now. I've – I've an appointment.' And he left me.

Had not my eyes been held I might have known that that broken muttering over the fire was the swansong of Charlie Mears. But I thought it the prelude to fuller revelation. At last and at last I should cheat the Lords of Life and Death!

When next Charlie came to me I received him with rapture. He was nervous and embarrassed, but his eyes were very full of light, and his lips a little parted.

'I've done a poem,' he said; and then, quickly: 'It's the best I've ever done. Read it.' He thrust it into my hand and retreated to the window.

I groaned inwardly. It would be the work of half an hour to criticise – that is to say, praise – the poem sufficiently to please Charlie. Then I had good reason to groan, for Charlie, discarding his favourite centipede metres, had launched into shorter and choppier verse, and verse with a motive at the back of it. This is what I read:–

The day is most fair, the cheery wind
    Halloos behind the hill,
Where he bends the wood as seemeth good,
    And the sapling to his will!
Riot, O wind; there is that in my blood
    That would not have thee still!

She gave me herself, O Earth, O Sky;
    Gray sea, she is mine alone!
Let the sullen boulders hear my cry,
    And rejoice tho' they be but stone!

Mine! I have won her, O good brown earth,
    Make merry! 'Tis hard on Spring;
Make merry; my love is doubly worth
    All worship your fields can bring!
Let the hind that tills you feel my mirth
    At the early harrowing!

'Yes, it's the early harrowing, past a doubt,' I said, with a dread at my heart. Charlie smiled, but did not answer.

Red cloud of the sunset, tell it abroad;
    I am victor. Greet me, O Sun,
Dominant master and absolute lord
    Over the soul of one!

'Well?' said Charlie, looking over my shoulder.

I thought it far from well, and very evil indeed, when he silently laid a photograph on the paper – the photograph of a girl with a curly head, and a foolish slack mouth.

'Isn't it – isn't it wonderful?' he whispered, pink to the tips of his ears, wrapped in the rosy mystery of first love. 'I didn't know; I didn't think – it came like a thunderclap.'

'Yes. It comes like a thunderclap. Are you very happy, Charlie?'

'My God – she – she loves me!' He sat down repeating the last words to himself. I looked at the hairless face, the narrow shoulders already bowed by desk-work, and wondered when, where, and how he had loved in his past lives.

'What will your mother say?' I asked cheerfully.

'I don't care a damn what she says!'

At twenty the things for which one does not care a damn should, properly, be many, but one must not include mothers in the list. I told him this gently; and he described Her, even as Adam must have described to the newly-named beasts the glory and tenderness and beauty of Eve. Incidentally I learned that She was a tobacconist's assistant with a weakness for pretty dress, and had told him four or five times already that She had never been kissed by a man before.

Charlie spoke on and on, and on; while I, separated from him by thousands of years, was considering the beginnings of things. Now I understood why the Lords of Life and Death shut the doors so carefully behind us. It is that we may not remember our first and most beautiful wooings. Were this not so, our world would be without inhabitants in a hundred years.

'Now, about that galley-story,' I said still more cheerfully, in a pause in the rush of the speech.

Charlie looked up as though he had been hit. 'The galley – what galley? Good heavens, don't joke, man! This is serious! You don't know how serious it is!'

Grish Chunder was right. Charlie had tasted the love of woman that kills remembrance, and the finest story in the world would never be written.

WHEN 'OMER SMOTE 'IS BLOOMIN' LYRE

WHEN 'Omer smote 'is bloomin' lyre,
   He'd 'eard men sing by land an' sea;
An' what he thought 'e might require,
   'E went an' took – the same as me!

The market-girls an' fishermen,
   The shepherds an' the sailors, too,
They 'eard old songs turn up again,
   But kep' it quiet – same as you!

They knew 'e stole; 'e knew they knowed.
   They didn't tell, nor make a fuss,
But winked at 'Omer down the road,
   An' 'e winked back – the same as us!

A LETTER TO THE *SPECTATOR*

YOUR article on 'Landscape and Literature' in the *Spectator* of June 18th has the following, among other suggestive passages: 'But whence came the vision of the enchanted island in *The Tempest?* It had no existence in Shakespeare's world, but was woven out of such stuff as dreams are made on.'

May I cite Malone's suggestion connecting the play with the casting away of Sir George Somers on the island of Bermuda in 1609? And further, may I be allowed to say how it seems to me possible that the vision was woven from the most prosaic material – from nothing more promising, in fact, than the chatter of a half-tipsy sailor at a theatre? Thus:–

A stage-manager, who writes and vamps plays, moving among his audience, overhears a mariner discoursing to his neighbour of a grievous wreck, and of the behaviour of the passengers, for whom all sailors have ever entertained a natural contempt. He describes, with the wealth of detail peculiar to sailors, measures taken to claw the ship off a lee-shore, how helm and sails were worked, what the passengers did, and what he said. One pungent phrase – to be rendered later into: 'What cares these roarers for the name of king?' – strikes the manager's ear, and he stands behind the talkers. Perhaps only one-tenth of the earnestly delivered, hand-on-shoulder sea-talk was actually used of all that was automatically and unconsciously stored by the inland man who knew all inland arts and crafts. Nor is it too fanciful to imagine a half-turn to the second listener as the mariner, banning his luck as mariners will, says there are those who would not give a doit to a poor man, while they will lay out ten to see a raree-show – a dead Indian. Were he in foreign parts, as now he is in England, he could show people something in the way of strange fish. Is it to consider too curiously to see a drink ensue on this hint (the manager dealt but little in his plays with the sea at first hand, and his instinct for new words would have been waked by what he had already caught), and with the drink a sailor's minute description of how he went across through the reefs to the island of his calamity – or islands rather, for there were many? Some you could almost carry away in your pocket. They were sown broadcast like – like the nutshells on the stage there. 'Many islands, in truth,' says the manager patiently, and afterwards his Sebastian says to Antonio: 'I think he will carry this island home in his pocket and give it his son for an apple.' To which Antonio answers: 'And, sowing the kernels of it in the sea, bring forth more islands.'

'But what was the land like?' says the manager. The sailor tries to explain. 'It was green, with yellow in it; a tawny-coloured country,' – the colour, that is to say, of the coral-beached, cedar-covered Bermuda of today – 'and the air made one sleepy, and the place was full of noises' – the muttering and roaring of the sea among the islands and between the reefs – 'and there was a sou'-west wind that blistered one all over'. The Elizabethan mariner would not distinguish finely between blisters and prickly heat; but the Bermudian of to-day will tell you that the sou'-west or Lighthouse wind in summer brings that plague and general discomfort. That the coral rock, battered by the sea, rings hollow with strange sounds, answered by the winds in the little cramped valleys, is a matter of common knowledge.

The man, refreshed with more drink, then describes the geography of his landing-place – the spot where Trinculo makes his first appearance. He insists and reinsists on details which to him at one time meant life or death; and the manager follows attentively. He can give his audience no more than a few hangings and a placard for scenery, but – that his lines should lift them beyond that bare show to the place he would have them – the manager needs for himself the clearest possible understanding – the most ample detail. He must see the scene in the round – solid – ere he peoples it. Much, doubtless, he discarded, but so closely did he keep to his original information that those who go today to a certain beach some two miles from

Hamilton will find the stage set for Act II. Scene 2 of *The Tempest* – a bare beach, with the wind singing through the scrub at the land's edge, a gap in the passage wide enough for Stephano's butt of sack, and (these eyes have seen it) a cave in the coral within easy reach of the tide, whereto such a butt might be conveniently rolled ('My cellar is in a rock by the seaside where my wine is hid'). There is no other cave for some two miles. 'Here's neither bush or shrub'; one is exposed to the wrath of 'yond same black cloud', and here the currents strand wreckage. It was so well done that, after three hundred years, a stray tripper, and no Shakespeare scholar, recognised in a flash that old first set of all.

So far good. Up to this point the manager has gained little except some suggestions for an opening scene, and some notion of an uncanny island. The mariner (one cannot believe that Shakespeare was mean in these little things) is dipping to a deeper drunkenness. Suddenly he launches into a preposterous tale of himself and his fellows, flung ashore, separated from their officers, horribly afraid of the devil-haunted beach of noises, with their heads full of the fumes of broached liquor. One castaway was found hiding under the ribs of a dead whale, which smelt abominably. They hauled him out by the legs, – he mistook them for imps – and gave him drink. And now, discipline being melted, they would strike out for themselves, defy their officers, and take possession of the island. The narrator's mates in this enterprise were probably described as fools. He was the only sober man in the company.

So they went inland, faring badly as they went up and down this pestilent country. They were pricked with palmettoes, and the cedar branches rasped their faces. Then they found and stole some of their officers' clothes, which were hanging up to dry. But presently they fell into a swamp, and, what was worse, into the hands of their officers; and the great expedition ended in muck and mire. Truly an island bewitched. Else why their cramps and sickness? Sack never made a man more than reasonably drunk. He was prepared to answer for unlimited sack; but what befell his stomach and head was the purest magic that honest man ever met.

A drunken sailor of today wandering about Bermuda would probably sympathise with him; and today, as then, if one takes the easiest inland road from Trinculo's beach, near Hamilton, the path that a drunken man would infallibly follow, it ends abruptly in a swamp. The one point that our mariner did not dwell upon was that he and the others were suffering from acute alcoholism combined with the effects of nerve-shattering peril and exposure. Hence the magic. That a wizard should control such an island was demanded by the beliefs of all seafarers of that date.

Accept this theory, and you will concede that *The Tempest* came to the manager sanely and normally in the course of his daily life. He may have been casting about for a new play. he may have purposed to vamp an old one – say *Aurelio and Isabella*. Or he may have been merely waiting on his Demon. But it is Prospero's wealth against Caliban's pignuts that to him in a receptive hour, sent by Heaven, entered the original Stephano fresh from the seas and half-seas-over. To him Stephano told his tale all in one piece, a two hours' discourse of most glorious absurdities. His profligate abundance of detail at the beginning, when he was more or less sober, supplied and surely established the earth-basis of the play in accordance with the great law that a story to be truly miraculous must be ballasted with facts. His maunderings of magic and incomprehensible ambushings, when he was without reservation drunk (and this is just the time when a lesser-minded man than Shakespeare would have paid the reckoning and turned him out), suggested to the manager the peculiar note of its supernatural mechanism.

Truly it was a dream, but that there may be no doubt of its source or of his obligation, Shakespeare has also made the dreamer immortal!

'WIRELESS'

'IT'S a funny thing, this Marconi business, isn't it?' said Mr Shaynor, coughing heavily. 'Nothing seems to make any difference, by what they tell me – storms, hills or anything; but if that's true we shall know before morning.'

'Of course it's true,' I answered, stepping behind the counter. 'Where's old Mr Cashell?'

'He's had to go to bed on account of his influenza. He said you'd very likely drop in.'

'Where's his nephew?'

'Inside, getting the things ready. He told me that the last time they experimented they put the pole on the roof of one of the big hotels here, and the batteries electrified all the water-supply, and' – he giggled – 'the ladies got shocks when they took their baths.'

'I never heard of that.'

'The hotel wouldn't exactly advertise it, would it? Just now, by what Mr Cashell tells me, they're trying to signal from here to Poole, and they're using stronger batteries than ever. But, you see, he being the guvnor's nephew and all that (and it will be in the papers too), it doesn't matter how they electrify things in this house. Are you going to watch?'

'Very much. I've never seen this game. Aren't you going to bed?'

'We don't close till ten on Saturdays. There's a good deal of influenza in town, too, and there'll be a dozen prescriptions coming in before morning. I generally sleep in the chair here. It's warmer than jumping out of bed every time. Bitter cold, isn't it?'

'Freezing hard. I'm sorry your cough's worse.'

'Thank you. I don't mind cold so much. It's this wind that fair cuts me to pieces.' He coughed again hard and hackingly, as an old lady came in for ammoniated quinine. 'We've just run out of it in bottles, madam,' said Mr Shaynor, returning to the professional tone, 'but if you will wait two minutes, I'll make it up for you, madam.'

I had used the shop for some time, and my acquaintance with the proprietor had ripened into friendship. It was Mr Cashell who revealed to me the purpose and power of Apothecaries' Hall what time a fellow-chemist had made an error in a prescription of mine, had lied to cover his sloth, and when error and lie were brought home to him had written vain letters.

'A disgrace to our profession,' said the thin, mild-eyed man, hotly, after studying the evidence. 'You couldn't do a better service to the profession than report him to Apothecaries' Hall.'

I did so, not knowing what djinns I should evoke; and the result was such an apology as one might make who had spent a night on the rack. I conceived great respect for Apothecaries' Hall, and esteem for Mr Cashell, a zealous craftsman who magnified his calling. Until Mr Shaynor came down from the North his assistants had by no means agreed with Mr Cashell. 'They forget,' said he, 'that, first and foremost, the compounder is a medicine-man. On him depends the physician's reputation. He holds it literally in the hollow of his hand, Sir.'

Mr Shaynor's manners had not, perhaps, the polish of the grocery and Italian warehouse next door, but he knew and loved his dispensary work in every detail. For relaxation he seemed to go no farther afield than the romance of drugs – their discovery, preparation, packing, and export – but it led him to the ends of the earth, and on this subject, and the Pharmaceutical Formulary, and Nicholas Culpepper, most confident of physicians, we met.

Little by little I grew to know something of his beginnings and his hopes – of his mother, who had been a school-teacher in one of the northern counties, and of his red-headed father, a small job-master at Kirby Moors, who died when he was a child; of the examinations he had passed and of their exceeding and increasing difficulty; of his dreams of a shop in London; of his hate for the price-cutting Co-operative stores; and, most interesting, of his mental attitude towards customers.

'There's a way you get into,' he told me, 'of serving them carefully, and I hope, politely, without stopping your own thinking. I've been reading Christie's *New Commercial Plants* all this autumn, and that needs keeping your mind on it, I can tell you. So long as it isn't a prescription, of course, I can carry as much as half a page of Christie in my head, and at the same time I could sell out all that window twice over, and not a penny wrong at the end. As to prescriptions, I think I could make up the general run of 'em in my sleep, almost.'

For reasons of my own, I was deeply interested in Marconi experiments at their outset in England; and it was of a piece with Mr Cashell's unvarying thoughtfulness that, when his nephew the electrician appropriated the house for a long-range installation, he should, as I have said, invite me to see the result.

The old lady went away with her medicine, and Mr Shaynor and I stamped on the tiled floor behind the counter to keep ourselves warm. The shop, by the light of the many electrics, looked like a Paris-diamond mine, for Mr Cashell believed in all the ritual of his craft. Three superb glass jars – red, green, and blue – of the sort that led Rosamund to parting with her shoes – blazed in the broad plate-glass windows, and there was a confused smell of orris, Kodak films, vulcanite, tooth-powder, sachets, and almond-cream in the air. Mr Shaynor fed the dispensary stove, and we sucked cayenne-pepper jujubes and menthol lozenges. The brutal east wind had cleared the streets, and the few passers-by were muffled to their puckered eyes. In the Italian warehouse next door some gay feathered birds and game, hung over hooks, sagged to the wind across the left edge of our window-frame.

'They ought to take these poultry in – all knocked about like that,' said Mr Shaynor. 'Doesn't it make you feel fair perishing? See that old hare! The wind's nearly blowing the fur off him.'

I saw the belly-fur of the dead beast blown apart in ridges and streaks as the wind caught it, showing bluish skin underneath.

'Bitter cold,' said Mr Shaynor, shuddering. 'Fancy going out on a night like this! Oh, here's young Mr Cashell.'

The door of the inner office behind the dispensary opened, and an energetic, spade-bearded man stepped forth, rubbing his hands.

'I want a bit of tin-foil, Shaynor,' he said. 'Good-evening. My uncle told me you might be coming.' This to me, as I began the first of a hundred questions.

'I've everything in order,' he replied. 'We're only waiting until Poole calls us up. Excuse me a minute. You can come in whenever you like – but I'd better be with the instruments. Give me that tin-foil. Thanks.'

While we were talking, a girl – evidently no customer – had come into the shop, and the face and bearing of Mr Shaynor changed. She leaned confidently across the counter.

'But I can't,' I heard him whisper uneasily – the flush on his cheek was dull red, and his eyes shone like a drugged moth's. 'I can't. I tell you I'm alone in the place.'

'No, you aren't. Who's *that*? Let him look after it for half an hour. A brisk walk will do you good. Ah, come now, John.'

'But he isn't – '

'I don't care. I want you to; we'll only go round by St. Agnes. If you don't – '

He crossed to where I stood in the shadow of the dispensary counter, and began some sort of broken apology about a lady-friend.

'Yes,' she interrupted. 'You take the shop for half an hour – to oblige *me*, won't you?'

She had a singularly rich and promising voice that well matched her outline.

'All right,' I said. 'I'll do it – but you'd better wrap yourself up, Mr Shaynor.'

'Oh, a brisk walk ought to help me. We're only going round by the church.' I heard him cough grievously as they went out together.

I refilled the stove, and, after reckless expenditure of Mr Cashell's coal, drove some warmth into the shop. I explored many of the glass-knobbed drawers that lined the walls, tasted some disconcerting drugs, and, by the aid of a few cardamoms, ground ginger, chloric-ether, and dilute alcohol, manufactured a new and wildish drink, of which I bore a glassful to young Mr Cashell, busy in the back office. He laughed shortly when I told him that Mr Shaynor had stepped out – but a frail coil of wire held all his attention, and he had no word for me bewildered among the batteries and rods. The noise of the sea on the beach began to make itself heard as the traffic in the street ceased. Then briefly, but very lucidly, he gave me the names and uses of the mechanism that crowded the tables and the floor.

'When do you expect to get the message from Poole?' I demanded, sipping my liquor out of a graduated glass.

'About midnight, if everything is in order. We've got our installation-pole fixed to the roof of the house. I shouldn't advise you to turn on a tap or anything to-night. We've connected up with the plumbing, and all the water will be electrified.' He repeated to me the history of the agitated ladies at the hotel at the time of the first installation.

'But what *is* it?' I asked. 'Electricity is out of my beat altogether.'

'Ah, if you knew *that* you'd know something nobody knows. It's just It – what we call Electricity, but the magic – the manifestations – the Hertzian waves – are all revealed by *this*. The coherer, we call it.'

He picked up a glass tube not much thicker than a thermometer, in which, almost touching, were two tiny silver plugs, and between them an infinitesimal pinch of metallic dust. 'That's all,' he said, proudly, as though himself responsible for the wonder. 'That is the thing that will reveal to us the Powers – whatever the Powers may be – at work – through space – a long distance away.'

Just then Mr Shaynor returned alone and stood coughing his heart out on the mat.

'Serves you right for being such a fool,' said young Mr Cashell, as annoyed as myself at the interruption. 'Never mind – we've all the night before us to see wonders.'

Shaynor clutched the counter, his handkerchief to his lips. When he brought it away I saw two bright red stains.

'I – I've got a bit of a rasped throat from smoking cigarettes,' he panted. 'I think I'll try a cubeb.'

'Better take some of this. I've been compounding while you've been away.' I handed him the brew.

''Twon't make me drunk, will it? I'm almost a teetotaller. My word! That's grateful and comforting.'

He set down the empty glass to cough afresh.

'Brr! But it was cold out there! I shouldn't care to be lying in my grave a night like this. Don't *you* ever have a sore throat from smoking?' He pocketed the handkerchief after a furtive peep.

'Oh, yes sometimes,' I replied, wondering, while I spoke, into what agonies of terror I should fall if ever I saw those bright-red danger-signals under my nose. Young Mr Cashell among the batteries coughed slightly to show that he was quite ready to continue his scientific explanation, but I was thinking still of the girl with the rich voice and the significantly cut mouth, at whose command I had taken charge of the shop. It flashed across me that she distantly resembled the seductive shape on a gold-framed toilet-water advertisement whose charms were unholily heightened by the glare from the red bottle in the window. Turning to make sure, I saw Mr Shaynor's eyes bent in the same direction, and by instinct recognised that the flamboyant thing was to him a shrine. 'What do you take for your – cough?' I asked.

'Well, I'm the wrong side of the counter to believe much in patent medicines. But there are asthma cigarettes and there are pastilles. To tell you the truth, if you don't object to the smell, which is very like incense, I believe, though I'm not a Roman Catholic, Blaudett's Cathedral Pastilles relieve me as much as anything.'

'Let's try.' I had never raided a chemist's shop before, so I was thorough. We unearthed the pastilles – brown, gummy cones of benzoin – and set them alight under the toilet-water advertisement, where they fumed in thin blue spirals.

'Of course,' said Mr Shaynor, to my question, 'what one uses in the shop for one's self comes out of one's pocket. Why, stock-taking in our business is nearly the same as with

jewellers – and I can't say more than that. But one gets them'
– he pointed to the pastille-box – 'at trade prices.' Evidently
the censing of the gay, seven-tinted wench with the teeth was
an established ritual which cost something.

'And when do we shut up shop?'

'We stay like this all night. The guv – old Mr Cashell –
doesn't believe in locks and shutters as compared with electric
light. Besides, it brings trade. I'll just sit here in the chair by
the stove and write a letter, if you don't mind. Electricity isn't
my prescription.'

The energetic young Mr Cashell snorted within, and Shaynor
settled himself up in his chair over which he had thrown a
staring red, black, and yellow Austrian jute blanket, rather like
a table-cover. I cast about, amid patent-medicine pamphlets,
for something to read, but finding little, returned to the
manufacture of the new drink. The Italian warehouse took
down its game and went to bed. Across the street blank shutters
flung back the gaslight in cold smears; the dried pavement
seemed to rough up in goose-flesh under the scouring of
the savage wind, and we could hear, long ere he passed, the
policeman flapping his arms to keep himself warm. Within,
the flavours of cardamoms and chloric-ether disputed those of
the pastilles and a score of drugs and perfume and soap scents.
Our electric lights, set low down in the windows before the tun-
bellied Rosamund jars, flung inward three monstrous daubs
of red, blue, and green, that broke into kaleidoscopic lights
on the facetted knobs of the drug-drawers, the cut-glass scent
flagons, and the bulbs of the sparklet bottles. They flushed
the white-tiled floor in gorgeous patches; splashed along the
nickel-silver counter-rails, and turned the polished mahogany
counter-panels to the likeness of intricate grained marbles
– slabs of porphyry and malachite. Mr Shaynor unlocked
a drawer, and ere he began to write, took out a meagre
bundle of letters. From my place by the stove, I could see the
scalloped edges of the paper with a flaring monogram in the
corner and could even smell the reek of chypre. At each page
he turned toward the toilet-water lady of the advertisement
and devoured her with over-luminous eyes. He had drawn the

Austrian blanket over his shoulders, and among those warring lights he looked more than ever the incarnation of a drugged moth – a tiger-moth as I thought.

He put his letter into an envelope, stamped it with stiff mechanical movements, and dropped it in the drawer. Then I became aware of the silence of a great city asleep – the silence that underlaid the even voice of the breakers along the sea-front – a thick, tingling quiet of warm life stilled down for its appointed time, and unconsciously I moved about the glittering shop as one moves in a sick-room. Young Mr Cashell was adjusting some wire that crackled from time to time with the tense, knuckle-stretching sound of the electric spark. Upstairs, where a door shut and opened swiftly, I could hear his uncle coughing abed.

'Here,' I said, when the drink was properly warmed, 'take some of this, Mr Shaynor.'

He jerked in his chair with a start and a wrench, and held out his hand for the glass. The mixture, of a rich port-wine colour, frothed at the top.

'It looks,' he said, suddenly, 'it looks – those bubbles – like a string of pearls winking at you – rather like the pearls round that young lady's neck.' He turned again to the advertisement where the female in the dove-coloured corset had seen fit to put on all her pearls before she cleaned her teeth.

'Not bad, is it?' I said.

'Eh?'

He rolled his eyes heavily full on me, and, as I stared, I beheld all meaning and consciousness die out of the swiftly dilating pupils. His figure lost its stark rigidity, softened into the chair, and, chin on chest, hands dropped before him, he rested open-eyed, absolutely still.

'I'm afraid I've rather cooked Shaynor's goose,' I said, bearing the fresh drink to young Mr Cashell. 'Perhaps it was the chloric-ether.'

'Oh, he's all right.' The spade-bearded man glanced at him pityingly. 'Consumptives go off in those sort of dozes very often. It's exhaustion . . . I don't wonder. I daresay the liquor will do him good. It's grand stuff,' he finished his share appreciatively. 'Well, as I was saying – before he interrupted – about this little coherer. The pinch of dust, you see, is nickel-filings. The Hertzian waves, you see, come out of space from the station that despatches 'em, and all these little particles are attracted together – cohere, we call it – for just so long as the current passes through them. Now, it's important to remember that the current is an induced current. There are a good many kinds of induction – '

'Yes, but what *is* induction?'

'That's rather hard to explain untechnically. But the long and short of it is that when a current of electricity passes through a wire there's a lot of magnetism present round that wire; and if you put another wire parallel to, and within what we call its magnetic field – why then, the second wire will also become charged with electricity.'

'On its own account?'

'On its own account.'

'Then let's see if I've got it correctly. Miles off, at Poole, or wherever it is – '

'It will be anywhere in ten years.'

'You've got a charged wire – '

'Charged with Hertzian waves which vibrate, say, two hundred and thirty million times a second.' Mr Cashell snaked his forefinger rapidly through the air.

'All right – a charged wire at Poole, giving out these waves into space. Then this wire of yours sticking out into space – on the roof of the house – in some mysterious way gets charged with those waves from Poole – '

'Or anywhere – it only happens to be Poole to-night.'

'And those waves set the coherer at work, just like an ordinary telegraph-office ticker?'

'No! That's where so many people make the mistake. The Hertzian waves wouldn't be strong enough to work a great heavy Morse instrument like ours. They can only just make that dust cohere, and while it coheres (a little while for a dot and a longer while for a dash) the current from this battery – the home battery' – he laid his hand on the thing – 'can get through to the Morse printing-machine to record the dot or dash. Let me make it clearer. Do you know anything about steam?'

'Very little. But go on.'

'Well, the coherer is like a steam-valve. Any child can open a valve and start a steamer's engines, because a turn of the hand lets in the main steam, doesn't it? Now, this home battery here ready to print is the main steam. The coherer is the valve, always ready to be turned on. The Hertzian wave is the child's hand that turns it.'

'I see. That's marvellous.'

'Marvellous, isn't it? And, remember, we're only at the beginning. There's nothing we shan't be able to do in ten years. I want to live – my God, how I want to live, and see it develop?' He looked through the door at Shaynor breathing lightly in his chair. 'Poor beast! And he wants to keep company with Fanny Brand.'

'Fanny *who*?' I said, for the name struck an obscurely familiar chord in my brain – something connected with a stained handkerchief, and the word 'arterial'.

'Fanny Brand – the girl you kept shop for.' He laughed. 'That's all I know about her, and for the life of me I can't see what Shaynor sees in her, or she in him.'

'*Can't* you see what he sees in her?' I insisted.

'Oh, yes, if *that's* what you mean. She's a great, big, fat lump of a girl, and so on. I suppose that's why he's so crazy after her. She isn't his sort. Well, it doesn't matter. My uncle says he's bound to die before the year's out. Your drink's given him a good sleep, at any rate.' Young Mr Cashell could not catch Mr Shaynor's face, which was half turned to the advertisement.

I stoked the stove anew, for the room was growing cold, and lighted another pastille. Mr Shaynor in his chair, never moving, looked through and over me with eyes as wide and lustreless as those of a dead hare.

'Poole's late,' said young Mr Cashell, when I stepped back. 'I'll just send them a call.'

He pressed a key in the semi-darkness, and with a rending

crackle there leaped between two brass knobs a spark, streams of sparks and sparks again.

'Grand, isn't it? *That's* the Power – or unknown Power – kicking and fighting to be let loose,' said young Mr Cashell. 'There she goes – kick – kick – kick into space. I never get over the strangeness of it when I work a sending-machine – waves going into space, you know. T R is our call. Poole ought to answer with L L L.'

We waited two, three, five minutes. In that silence, of which the boom of the tide was an orderly part, I caught the clear '*kiss – kiss – kiss*' of the halliards on the roof, as they were blown against the installation-pole.

'Poole is not ready. I'll stay here and call you when he is.'

I returned to the shop, and set down my glass on a marble slab with a careless clink. As I did so, Shaynor rose to his feet, his eyes fixed once more on the advertisement, where the young woman bathed in the light from the red jar simpered pinkly over her pearls. His lips moved without cessation. I stepped nearer to listen. 'And threw – and threw – and threw,' he repeated, his face all sharp with some inexplicable agony.

I moved forward astonished. But it was then he found words – delivered roundly and clearly. These:–

And threw warm gules on Madeleine's young breast.

The trouble passed off his countenance, and he returned lightly to his place, rubbing his hands.

It had never occurred to me, though we had many times discussed reading and prize-competitions as a diversion, that Mr Shaynor ever read Keats, or could quote him at all appositely. There was, after all, a certain stained-glass effect of light on the high bosom of the highly-polished picture which might, by stretch of fancy, suggest, as a vile chromo recalls some incomparable canvas, the line he had spoken. Night, my drink, and solitude were evidently turning Mr Shaynor into a poet. He sat down again and wrote swiftly on his villainous note-paper, his lips quivering.

I shut the door into the inner office and moved up behind

him. He made no sign that he saw or heard. I looked over his shoulder, and read, amid half-formed words, sentences, and wild scratches:-

> – Very cold it was. Very cold
> The hare – the hare – the hare –
> The birds –

He raised his head sharply, and frowned toward the blank shutters of the poulterer's shop where they jutted out against our window. Then one clear line came:-

> The hare, in spite of fur, was very cold.

The head, moving machine-like, turned right to the advertisement where the Blaudett's Cathedral pastille reeked abominably. He grunted, and went on:–

> Incense in a censer –
> Before her darling picture framed in gold –
> Maiden's picture – angel's portrait –

'Hsh!' said Mr Cashell guardedly from the inner office, as though in the presence of spirits. 'There's something coming through from somewhere; but it isn't Poole.' I heard the crackle of sparks as he depressed the keys of the transmitter. In my own brain, too, something crackled, or it might have been the hair on my head. Then I heard my own voice, in a harsh whisper: 'Mr Cashell, there is something coming through here, too. Leave me alone till I tell you.'

'But I thought you'd come to see this wonderful thing – Sir,' indignantly at the end.

'Leave me alone till I tell you. Be quiet.'

I watched – I waited. Under the blue-veined hand – the dry hand of the consumptive – came away clear, without erasure:-

> And my weak spirit fails
> To think how the dead must freeze –

he shivered as he wrote –

> Beneath the churchyard mould.

Then he stopped, laid the pen down, and leaned back.

For an instant, that was half an eternity, the shop spun before me in a rainbow-tinted whirl, in and through which my own soul most dispassionately considered my own soul as that fought with an over-mastering fear. Then I smelt the strong smell of cigarettes from Mr Shaynor's clothing, and heard, as though it had been the rending of trumpets, the rattle of his breathing. I was still in my place of observation, much as one would watch a rifle-shot at the butts, half-bent, hands on my knees, and head within a few inches of the black, red, and yellow blanket of his shoulder. I was whispering encouragement, evidently to my other self, sounding sentences, such as men pronounce in dreams.

'If he had read Keats, it proves nothing. If he hasn't – like causes *must* beget like effects. There is no escape from this law. *You* ought to be grateful that you know "St Agnes' Eve" without the book; because, given the circumstances, such as Fanny Brand, who is the key of the enigma, and approximately represents the latitude and longitude of Fanny Brawne; allowing also for the bright red colour of the arterial blood upon the handkerchief, which was just what you were puzzling over in the shop just now; and counting the effect of the professional environment, here almost perfectly duplicated – the result is logical and inevitable. As inevitable as induction.'

Still, the other half of my soul refused to be comforted. It was cowering in some minute and inadequate corner – at an immense distance.

Hereafter, I found myself one person again, my hands still gripping my knees, and my eyes glued on the page before Mr Shaynor. As dreamers accept and explain the upheaval of landscapes and the resurrection of the dead, with excerpts from the evening hymn or the multiplication-table, so I had accepted the facts, whatever they might be, that I should witness, and had devised a theory, sane and plausible to my mind, that explained them all. Nay, I was even in advance of my facts, walking hurriedly before them, assured that they would fit my theory. And all that I now recall of that epoch-making theory are the lofty words: 'If he has read Keats it's the chloric-ether. If he hasn't, it's the identical bacillus, or Hertzian wave of tuberculosis, *plus* Fanny Brand and the professional status which, in conjunction with the main-stream of subconscious thought common to all mankind, has thrown up temporarily an induced Keats.'

Mr Shaynor returned to his work, erasing and rewriting as before with swiftness. Two or three blank pages he tossed aside. Then he wrote, muttering:–

The little smoke of a candle that goes out.

'No,' he muttered. 'Little smoke – little smoke – little smoke. What else?' He thrust his chin forward toward the advertisement, whereunder the last of the Blaudett's Cathedral pastilles fumed in its holder. 'Ah!' Then with relief:–

The little smoke that dies in moonlight cold.

Evidently he was snared by the rhymes of his first verse, for he wrote and rewrote 'gold – cold – mould' many times. Again he sought inspiration from the advertisement, and set down, without erasure, the line I had overheard:–

And threw warm gules on Madeleine's young breast.

As I remembered the original it is 'fair' – a trite word – instead of 'young', and I found myself nodding approval, though I admitted that the attempt to reproduce 'its little smoke in pallid moonlight died' was a failure.

Followed without a break ten or fifteen lines of bald prose – the naked soul's confession of its physical yearning for its beloved – unclean as we count uncleanliness; unwholesome, but human exceedingly; the raw material, so it seemed to me in that hour and in that place, whence Keats wove the twenty-sixth, seventh, and eighth stanzas of his poem. Shame I had none in overseeing this revelation; and my fear had gone with the smoke of the pastille.

'That's it,' I murmured. 'That's how it's blocked out. Go on! Ink it in, man. Ink it in!'

Mr Shaynor returned to broken verse wherein 'loveliness' was made to rhyme with a desire to look upon 'her empty dress'. He picked up a fold of the gay, soft blanket, spread it over one hand, caressed it with infinite tenderness, thought, muttered, traced some snatches which I could not decipher, shut his eyes drowsily, shook his head, and dropped the stuff. Here I found myself at fault, for I could not then see (as I do now) in what manner a red, black, and yellow Austrian blanket coloured his dreams.

In a few minutes he laid aside his pen, and, chin on hand, considered the shop with thoughtful and intelligent eyes. He threw down the blanket, rose, passed along a line of drug-drawers, and read the names on the labels aloud. Returning, he took from his desk Christie's *New Commercial Plants* and the old Culpepper that I had given him, opened and laid them side by side with a clerky air, all trace of passion gone from his face, read first in one and then in the other, and paused with pen behind his ear.

'What wonder of Heaven's coming now?' I thought.

'Manna – manna – manna,' he said at last, under wrinkled brows. 'That's what I wanted. Good! Now then! Now then! Good! Good! Oh, by God, that's good!' His voice rose and he spoke rightly and fully without a falter:–

> Candied apple, quince and plum and gourd,
> And jellies smoother than the creamy curd,
> And lucent syrups tinct with cinnamon,
> Manna and dates in Argosy transferred
> From Fez; and spiced dainties, every one
> From silken Samarcand to cedared Lebanon.

He repeated it once more, using 'blander' for 'smoother' in the second line; then wrote it down without erasure, but this time (my set eyes missed no stroke of any word) he substituted 'soother' for his atrocious second thought, so that it came away under his hand as it is written in the book – as it is written in the book.

A wind went shouting down the street, and on the heels of the wind followed a spurt and rattle of rain.

After a smiling pause – and good right had he to smile – he began anew, always tossing the last sheet over his shoulder:–

> The sharp rain falling on the window-pane,
> Rattling sleet – the wind-blown sleet.

Then prose: 'It is very cold of mornings when the wind brings rain and sleet with it. I heard the sleet on the window-pane outside, and thought of you, my darling. I am always thinking of you. I wish we could both run away like two lovers into the storm and get that little cottage by the sea which we are always thinking about, my own dear darling. We could sit and watch the sea beneath our windows. It would be a fairyland all of our own – a fairy sea – a fairy sea . . .'

He stopped, raised his head, and listened. The steady drone of the Channel along the seafront that had borne us company so long leaped up a note to the sudden fuller surge that signals the change from ebb to flood. It beat in like the change of step throughout an army – this renewed pulse of the sea – and filled our ears till they, accepting it, marked it no longer.

> A fairyland for you and me
> Across the foam – beyond . . .
> A magic foam, a perilous sea.

He grunted again with effort and bit his underlip. My throat dried, but I dared not gulp to moisten it lest I should break the spell that was drawing him nearer and nearer to the highwater mark but two of the sons of Adam have reached. Remember that in all the millions permitted there are no more than five – five little lines – of which one can say: 'These are the pure

Magic. These are the clear Vision. The rest is only poetry.' And
Mr Shaynor was playing hot and cold with two of them!

I vowed no unconscious thought of mine should influence
the blindfold soul, and pinned myself desperately to the other
three, repeating and re-repeating:–

> A savage spot as holy and enchanted
> As e'er beneath a waning moon was haunted
> By woman wailing for her demon lover.

But though I believed my brain thus occupied, my every
sense hung upon the writing under the dry, bony hand, all
brown-fingered with chemicals and cigarette-smoke.

> Our windows fronting on the dangerous foam,

(he wrote, after long, irresolute snatches), and then –

> Our open casements facing desolate seas
> Forlorn – forlorn –

Here again his face grew peaked and anxious with that sense
of loss I had first seen when the Power snatched him. But this
time the agony was tenfold keener. As I watched it mounted
like mercury in the tube. It lighted his face from within till
I thought the visibly scourged soul must leap forth naked
between his jaws, unable to endure. A drop of sweat trickled
from my forehead down my nose and splashed on the back of
my hand.

> Our windows facing on the desolate seas
> And pearly foam of magic fairyland –

'Not yet – not yet,' he mutterd, 'wait a minute. *Please* wait
a minute. I shall get it then –

> Our magic windows fronting on the sea,
> The dangerous foam of desolate seas . . .
> For aye.

Ouh, my God!'

From head to heel he shook – shook from the marrow of his bones outwards – then leaped to his feet with raised arms, and slid the chair screeching across the tiled floor where it struck the drawers behind and fell with a jar. Mechanically, I stooped to recover it.

As I rose, Mr Shaynor was stretching and yawning at leisure.

'I've had a bit of a doze,' he said. 'How did I come to knock the chair over? You look rather – '

'The chair startled me,' I answered. 'It was so sudden in this quiet.'

Young Mr Cashell behind his shut door was offendedly silent.

'I suppose I must have been dreaming,' said Mr Shaynor.

'I suppose you must,' I said. 'Talking of dreams – I – I noticed you writing – before – '

He flushed consciously.

'I meant to ask you if you've ever read anything written by a man called Keats.'

'Oh! I haven't much time to read poetry, and I can't say that I remember the name exactly. Is he a popular writer?'

'Middling. I thought you might know him because he's the only poet who was ever a druggist. And he's rather what's called the lover's poet.'

'Indeed. I must dip into him. What did he write about?'

'A lot of things. Here's a sample that may interest you.'

Then and there, carefully, I repeated the verse he had twice spoken and once written not ten minutes ago.

'Ah! Anybody could see he was a druggist from that line about the tinctures and syrups. It's a fine tribute to our profession.'

'I don't know,' said young Mr Cashell, with icy politeness, opening the door one half-inch, 'if you still happen to be interested in our trifling experiments. But, should such be the case – '

I drew him aside, whispering, 'Shaynor seemed going off into some sort of fit when I spoke to you just now. I thought,

even at the risk of being rude, it wouldn't do to take you off
your instruments just as the call was coming through. Don't
you see?'

'Granted – granted as soon as asked,' he said, unbending.
'I *did* think it a shade odd at the time. So that was why he
knocked the chair down?'

'I hope I haven't missed anything,' I said.

'I'm afraid I can't say that, you're just in time for the end
of a rather curious performance. You can come in too, Mr
Shaynor. Listen, while I read it off.'

The Morse instrument was ticking furiously. Mr Cashell
interpreted: ' "*K K V. Can make nothing of your signals.*" '
A pause. ' "*M M V. M M V. Signals unintelligible. Purpose
anchor Sandown Bay. Examine instruments to-morrow.*" Do
you know what that means? It's a couple of men-o'-war
working Marconi signals off the Isle of Wight. They are trying
to talk to each other. Neither can read the other's messages,
but all their messages are being taken in by our receiver here.
They've been going on for ever so long. I wish you could have
heard it.'

'How wonderful!' I said. 'Do you mean we're overhearing
Portsmouth ships trying to talk to each other – that we're
eavesdropping across half South England?'

'Just that. Their transmitters are all right, but their receivers
are out of order, so they only get a dot here and a dash there.
Nothing clear.'

'Why is that?'

'God knows – and Science will know to-morrow. Perhaps the
induction is faulty; perhaps the receivers aren't tuned to receive
just the number of vibrations per second that the transmitter
sends. Only a word here and there. Just enough to tantalise.'

Again the Morse sprang to life.

'That's one of 'em complaining now. Listen: "*Disheartening
– most disheartening.*" It's quite pathetic. Have you ever seen
a spiritualistic seance? It reminds me of that sometimes – odds
and ends of messages coming out of nowhere – a word here and
there – no good at all.'

'But mediums are all impostors,' said Mr Shaynor, in the

doorway, lighting an asthma-cigarette. 'They only do it for the money they can make. I've seen 'em.'

'Here's Poole, at last – clear as a bell. L L L. *Now* we shan't be long.' Mr Cashell rattled the keys merrily. 'Anything you'd like to tell 'em?'

'No, I don't think so,' I said. 'I'll go home and get to bed. I'm feeling a little tired.'

LITERATURE

A great, and I frankly admit, a somewhat terrifying, honour has come to me; but I think, compliments apart, that the most case-hardened worker in letters, speaking to such an assembly as this, must recognise the gulf that separates even the least of those who do things worthy to be written about from even the best of those who have written things worthy of being talked about.

There is an ancient legend which tells us that when a man first achieved a most notable deed he wished to explain to his Tribe what he had done. As soon as he began to speak, however, he was smitten with dumbness, he lacked words, and sat down. Then there arose – according to the story – a masterless man, one who had taken no part in the action of his fellow, who had no special virtues, but who was afflicted – that is the phrase – with the magic of the necessary word. He saw; he told; he described the merits of the notable deed in such a fashion, we are assured, that the words 'became alive and walked up and down in the hearts of all his hearers'. Thereupon, the Tribe seeing that the words were certainly alive, and fearing lest the man with the words would hand down untrue tales about them to their children, took and killed him. But, later, they saw that the magic was in the words, not in the man.

We have progressed in many directions since the time of this early and destructive criticism, but, so far, we do not seem to have found a sufficient substitute for the necessary word as the final record to which all achievement must look. Even to-day, when all is done, those who have done it must wait until all has been said by the masterless man with the words. It is certain that the overwhelming bulk of those words will perish in the future as they have perished in the past; but it is true that a minute fraction will continue to exist, and by the light of these words, and by that light only, will our children be able to judge of the phases of our generation. Now we desire beyond all things to stand well with our children; but when our story comes to be told we do not know who will have the telling of it. We are too close to the tellers; there are many tellers and they are all talking together; and, even if we know them, we must not kill them. But the old and terrible instinct which taught our ancestors to kill the original story-teller warns us that we shall not be far wrong if we challenge any man who shows signs of being afflicted with the magic of the necessary word. May not this be the reason why, without any special legislation on its behalf, Literature has always stood a little outside the law as the one calling that is absolutely free – free in the sense that it needs no protection? For instance, if, as occasionally happens, a Judge makes a bad law, or a surgeon a bad operation, or a manufacturer makes bad food, criticism upon their actions is by law and custom confined to comparatively narrow limits. But if a man, as occasionally happens, makes a book, there is no limit to the criticism that may be directed against it. And this is perfectly as it should be. The world recognises that little things like bad law, bad surgery and bad food, affect only the cheapest commodity that we know about – human life. Therefore, in these circumstances, men can afford to be swayed by pity for the offender, by interest in his family, by fear, or loyalty, or respect for the organisation he represents, or even by a desire to do him justice. But when the question is of words – words that may become alive and walk up and down in the hearts of the hearers – it is then that this world of ours, which is disposed to take an interest in its future, feels instinctively that it is better that a thousand innocent people should be punished rather than that one guilty word should be preserved, carrying that which is an untrue tale of the Tribe. The chances, of course, are almost astronomically remote that any given tale will survive for so long as it takes an oak to grow to timber size. But that guiding instinct warns us not to trust to chance a matter of the supremest concern. In this durable record, if anything short of indisputable and undistilled truth be seen there, we all feel, 'How shall our achievements profit us?' The Record of the Tribe is its enduring literature.

The magic of Literature lies in the words, and not in any man. Witness, a thousand excellent, strenuous words can leave us quite cold or put us to sleep, whereas a bare half-hundred words breathed upon by some man in his agony, or in his exaltation, or in his idleness, ten generations ago, can still lead whole nations into and out of captivity, can open to us the doors of the three worlds, or stir us so intolerably that we can scarcely abide to look at our own souls. It is a miracle – one that happens very seldom. But secretly each one of the masterless men with the words has hope, or has had hope, that the miracle may be wrought again through him.

And why not? If a tinker in Bedford gaol; if a pamphleteering shopkeeper, pilloried in London; if a muzzy Scot; if a despised German Jew; or a condemned French thief, or an English Admiralty official with a taste for letters can be miraculously afflicted with the magic of the necessary word, why not any man at any time? Our world, which is only concerned in the perpetuation of the record, sanctions that hope just as kindly and just as cruelly as Nature sanctions love.

All it suggests is that the man with the Words shall wait upon the man of achievement, and step by step with him try to tell the story to the Tribe. All it demands is that the magic of every word shall be tried out to the uttermost by every means, fair or foul, that the mind of man can suggest. There is no room, and the world insists that there shall be no room, for pity, for mercy, for respect, for fear, or even for the loyalty between man and his fellow-man, when the record of the Tribe comes to be written. That record must satisfy, at all costs to the word and to the man behind the word. It must satisfy alike the keenest vanity and the deepest self-knowledge of the present; it must satisfy also the most shameless curiosity of the future. When it has done this it is literature of which it will be said, in due time, that it fitly represents its age. I say in due time because ages, like individuals, do not always appreciate the merits of a record that purports to represent them. The trouble is that one always expects just a little more out of a thing than

one puts into it. Whether it be an age or an individual, one
is always a little pained and a little pessimistic to find that all
one gets back is just one's bare deserts. This is a difficulty old
as literature.

A little incident that came within my experience a while ago
shows that that difficulty is always being raised by the most
unexpected people all about the world. It happened in a land
where the magic of words is peculiarly potent and far-reaching,
that there was a Tribe that wanted rain, and the rain-doctors
set about getting it. To a certain extent the rain-doctors
succeeded. But the rain their magic brought was not a full
driving downpour that tells of large prosperity; it was patchy,
local, circumscribed, and uncertain. There were unhealthy little
squalls blowing about the country and doing damage. Whole
districts were flooded out by waterspouts, and other districts
annoyed by trickling showers, soon dried by the sun. And
so the Tribe went to the rain-doctors, being very angry, and
they said 'What is this rain that you make? You did not make
rain like this in the time of our fathers. What have you been
doing?' And the rain-doctors said, 'We have been making our
proper magic. Supposing you tell us what you have been doing
lately?' And the Tribe said, 'Oh, our head-men have been
running about hunting jackals, and our little people have been
running about chasing grasshoppers! What has that to do with
your rain-making?' 'It has everything to do with it,' said the
rain-doctors. 'Just as long as your head-men run about hunting
jackals, and just as long your little people run about chasing
grasshoppers, just so long will the rain fall in this manner.'

THE FABULISTS

WHEN all the world would have a matter hid,
  Since Truth is seldom friend to any crowd,
Men write in fable, as old Aesop did,
  Jesting at that which none will name aloud.
And this they needs must do, or it will fall
Unless they please they are not heard at all.

When desperate Folly daily laboureth
  To work confusion upon all we have,
When diligent Sloth demandeth Freedom's death,
  And banded Fear commandeth Honour's grave –
Even in that certain hour before the fall,
Unless men please they are not heard at all.

Needs must all please, yet some not all for need,
  Needs must all toil, yet some not all for gain,
But that men taking pleasure may take heed,
  Whom present toil shall snatch from later pain.
Thus some have toiled but their reward was small
Since, though they pleased, they were not heard at all.

This was the lock that lay upon our lips,
  This was the yoke that we have undergone,
Denying us all pleasant fellowships
  As in our time and generation.
Our pleasures unpursued age past recall.
And for our pains – we are not heard at all.

What man hears aught except the groaning guns?
  What man heeds aught save what each instant brings?
When each man's life all imaged life outruns,
  What man shall pleasure in imaginings?
So it hath fallen, as it was bound to fall,
We are not, nor we were not, heard at all.

THE CRAFTSMAN

ONCE, after long-drawn revel at The Mermaid,
He to the overbearing Boanerges
Jonson, uttered (if half of it were liquor,
          Blessed be the vintage!)

Saying how, at an alehouse under Cotswold,
He had made sure of his very Cleopatra
Drunk with enormous, salvation-contemning
          Love for a tinker.

How, while he hid from Sir Thomas's keepers,
Crouched in a ditch and drenched by the midnight
Dews, he had listened to gipsy Juliet
          Rail at the dawning.

How at Bankside, a boy drowning kittens
Winced at the business; whereupon his sister –
Lady Macbeth aged seven – thrust 'em under,
          Sombrely scornful.

How on a Sabbath, hushed and compassionate –
She being known since her birth to the townsfolk –
Stratford dredged and delivered from Avon
          Dripping Ophelia.

So, with a thin third finger marrying
Drop to wine-drop domed on the table,
Shakespeare opened his heart till the sunrise
           Entered to hear him.

London waked and he, imperturbable,
Passed from waking to hurry after shadows . . .
Busied upon shows of no earthly importance?
           Yes, but he knew it!

THE BULL THAT THOUGHT

WESTWARD from a town by the Mouths of the Rhône, runs a road so mathematically straight, so barometrically level, that it ranks among the world's measured miles and motorists use it for records.

I had attacked the distance several times, but always with a Mistral blowing, or the unchancy cattle of those parts on the move. But once, running from the East, into a high-piled, almost Egyptian, sunset, there came a night which it would have been sin to have wasted. It was warm with the breath of summer in advance; moonlit till the shadow of every rounded pebble and pointed cypress wind-break lay solid on that vast flat-floored waste; and my Mr Leggatt, who had slipped out to make sure, reported that the road-surface was unblemished.

'*Now*,' he suggested, 'we might see what she'll do under strict road-conditions. She's been pullin' like the Blue de Luxe all day. Unless I'm all off, it's her night out.'

We arranged the trial for after dinner – thirty kilometres as near as might be; and twenty-two of them without even a level crossing.

There sat beside me at table d'hôte an elderly, bearded Frenchman wearing the rosette of by no means the lowest grade of the Legion of Honour, who had arrived in a talkative Citroën. I gathered that he had spent much of his life in the French Colonial Service in Annam and Tonquin. When the war came, his years barring him from the front line, he had supervised Chinese woodcutters who, with axe and dynamite, deforested the centre of France for trench-props. He said my chauffeur had told him that I contemplated an experiment. He was interested in cars – had admired mine – would, in short, be greatly indebted to me if I permitted him to assist as an observer. One could not well refuse; and, knowing my

Mr Leggatt, it occurred to me there might also be a bet in the background.

While he went to get his coat, I asked the proprietor his name. 'Voiron – Monsieur André Voiron,' was the reply. 'And his business?' 'Mon Dieu! He is Voiron! He is all those things, there!' The proprietor waved his hands at brilliant advertisements on the dining-room walls, which declared that Voiron Frères dealt in wines, agricultural implements, chemical manures, provisions and produce throughout that part of the globe.

He said little for the first five minutes of our trip, and nothing at all for the next ten – it being, as Leggatt had guessed, Esmeralda's night out. But, when her indicator climbed to a certain figure and held there for three blinding kilometres, he expressed himself satisfied, and proposed to me that we should celebrate the event at the hotel. 'I keep yonder,' said he, 'a wine on which I should value your opinion.'

On our return, he disappeared for a few minutes, and I heard him rumbling in a cellar. The proprietor presently invited me to the dining-room, where, beneath one frugal light, a table had been set with local dishes of renown. There was, too, a bottle beyond most known sizes, marked black on red, with a date. Monsieur Voiron opened it, and we drank to the health of my car. The velvety, perfumed liquor, between fawn and topaz, neither too sweet nor too dry, creamed in its generous glass. But I knew no wine composed of the whispers of angels' wings, the breath of Eden and the foam and pulse of Youth renewed. So I asked what it might be.

'It is champagne,' he said gravely.

'Then what have I been drinking all my life?'

'If you were lucky, before the War, and paid thirty shillings a bottle, it is possible you may have drunk one of our better-class *tisanes*.'

'And where does one get this?'

'Here, I am happy to say. Elsewhere, perhaps, it is not so easy. We growers exchange these real wines among ourselves.'

I bowed my head in admiration, surrender, and joy. There stood the most ample bottle, and it was not yet eleven o'clock. Doors locked and shutters banged throughout the establishment. Some last servant yawned on his way to bed. Monsieur Voiron opened a window and the moonlight flooded in from a small pebbled court outside. One could almost hear the town of Chambres breathing in its first sleep. Presently, there was a thick noise in the air, the passing of feet and hooves, lowings, and a stifled bark or two. Dust rose over the courtyard wall, followed by the strong smell of cattle.

'They are moving some beasts,' said Monsieur Voiron, cocking an ear. 'Mine, I think. Yes, I hear Christophe. Our beasts do not like automobiles – so we move at night. You do not know our country – the Crau, here, or the Camargue? I was – I am now, again – of it. All France is good; but this is the best.' He spoke, as only a Frenchman can, of his own loved part of his own lovely land.

'For myself, if I were not so involved in all these affairs' – he pointed to the advertisements – 'I would live on our farm with my cattle, and worship them like a Hindu. You know our cattle of the Camargue, Monsieur? No? It is not an acquaintance to rush upon lightly. There are no beasts like them. They have a mentality superior to that of others. They graze and they ruminate, by choice, facing our Mistral, which is more than some automobiles will do. Also they have in them the potentiality of thought – and when cattle think – I have seen what arrives.'

'Are they so clever as all that?' I asked idly.

'Monsieur, when your sportif chauffeur camouflaged your limousine so that she resembled one of your Army lorries, I would not believe her capacities. I bet him – ah – two to one – she would not touch ninety kilometres. It was proved that she could. I can give you no proof, but will you believe me if I tell you what a beast who thinks can achieve?'

'After the War,' said I spaciously, 'everything is credible.'

'That is true! Everything inconceivable has happened; but still we learn nothing and we believe nothing. When I was a child in my father's house – before I became a Colonial Administrator – my interest and my affection were among our cattle. We of the old rock live here – have you seen? –

in big farms like castles. Indeed, some of them may have been
Saracenic. The barns group round them – great white-walled
barns, and yards solid as our houses. One gate shuts all. It is
a world apart; an administration of all that concerns beasts.
It was there I learned something about cattle. You see, they
are our playthings in the Camargue and the Crau. The boy
measures his strength against the calf that butts him in play
among the manure-heaps. He moves in and out among the
cows, who are – not so amiable. He rides with the herdsmen
in the open to shift the herds. Sooner or later, he meets as
bulls the little calves that knocked him over. So it was with
me – till it became necessary that I should go to our Colonies.'
He laughed. 'Very necessary. That is a good time in youth,
Monsieur, when one does these things which shock our parents.
Why is it always Papa who is so shocked and has never heard
of such things – and Mamma who supplies the excuses? . . .
And when my brother – my elder who stayed and created the
business – begged me to return and help him, I resigned my
Colonial career gladly enough. I returned to our own lands, and
my well-loved, wicked white and yellow cattle of the Camargue
and the Crau. My Faith, I could talk of them all night, for
this stuff unlocks the heart, without making repentance in the
morning . . . Yes! It was after the War that this happened.
There was a calf, among Heaven knows how many of ours –
a bull-calf – an infant indistinguishable from his companions.
He was sick, and he had been taken up with his mother into
the big farmyard at home with us. Naturally the children of
our herdsman practised on him from the first. It is in their
blood. The Spaniards make a cult of bull-fighting. Our little
devils down here bait bulls as automatically as the English
child kicks or throws balls. This calf would chase them with
his eyes open, like a cow when she hunts a man. They would
take refuge behind our tractors and wine-carts in the centre of
the yard: he would chase them in and out as a dog hunts rats.
More than that, he would study their psychology, his eyes in
their eyes. Yes, he watched their faces to divine which way
they would run. He himself, also, would pretend sometimes
to charge directly at a boy. Then he would wheel right or left

– one could never tell – and knock over some child pressed
against a wall who thought himself safe. After this, he would
stand over him, knowing that his companions must come to his
aid; and when they were all together, waving their jackets across
his eyes and pulling his tail, he would scatter them – how he
would scatter them! He could kick, too, sideways like a cow. He
knew his ranges as well as our gunners, and he was as quick on
his feet as our Carpentier. I observed him often. Christophe –
the man who passed just now – our chief herdsman, who had
taught me to ride with our beasts when I was ten – Christophe
told me that he was descended from a yellow cow of those days
that had chased us once into the marshes. "He kicks just like
her," said Christophe. "He can side-kick as he jumps. Have
you seen, too, that he is not deceived by the jacket when a
boy waves it? He uses it to find the boy. They think they are
feeling him. He is feeling them always. He thinks, that one."
I had come to the same conclusion. Yes – the creature was a
thinker along the lines necessary to his sport; and he was a
humorist also, like so many natural murderers. One knows the
type among beasts as well as among men. It possesses a curious
truculent mirth – almost indecent but infallibly significant – '
    Monsieur Voiron replenished our glasses with the great wine
that went better at each descent.
    'They kept him for some time in the yards to practise upon.
Naturally he became a little brutal; so Christophe turned him
out to learn manners among his equals in the grazing lands,
where the Camargue joins the Crau. How old was he then?
About eight or nine months, I think. We met again a few
months later – he and I. I was riding one of our little
half-wild horses, along a road of the Crau, when I found
myself almost unseated. It was he! He had hidden himself
behind a wind-break till we passed, and had then charged my
horse from behind. But I recognised him. I gave him the whip
across the nose, and I said: "Apis, for this thou goest to Arles!
It was unworthy of thee, between us two." But that creature
had no shame. He went away laughing, like an Apache. If he
had dismounted me, I do not think it is I who would have
laughed – yearling as he was.'

'Why did you want to send him to Arles?' I asked.

'For the bull-ring. When your charming tourists leave us, we institute our little amusements there. Not a real bull-fight, you understand, but young bulls with padded horns, and our boys from hereabouts and in the city go to play with them. Naturally, before we send them we try them in our yards at home. So we brought up Apis from his pastures. He knew at once that he was among the friends of his youth – he almost shook hands with them – and he submitted like an angel to padding his horns. He investigated the carts and tractors in the yards, to choose his lines of defence and attack. And then – he attacked with an *elan*, and he defended with a tenacity and forethought that delighted us. In truth, we were so pleased that I fear we trespassed upon his patience. We desired him to repeat himself, which no true artist will tolerate. But he gave us fair warning. He went out to the centre of the yard, where there was some dry earth; he kneeled down and – you have seen a calf whose horns fret him thrusting and rooting into a bank? He did just that, very deliberately, till he had rubbed the pads off his horns. Then he rose, dancing on those wonderful feet that twinkled, and he said: "Now, my friends, the buttons are off the foils. Who begins?" We understood. We finished at once. He was turned out again on the pastures till it should be time to amuse them at our little metropolis. But, some time before he went to Arles – yes, I think I have it correctly – Christophe, who had been out on the Crau, informed me that Apis had assassinated a young bull who had given signs of developing into a rival. That happens, of course, and our herdsmen should prevent it. But Apis had killed in his own style – at dusk, from the ambush of a wind-break – by an oblique charge from behind which knocked the other over. He had then disembowelled him. All very possible, *but* – the murder accomplished – Apis went to the bank of a wind-break, knelt, and carefully, as he had in our yard, cleaned his horns in the earth. Christophe, who had never seen such a thing, at once borrowed (do you know, it is most efficacious when taken that way?) some Holy Water from our little chapel in those pastures, sprinkled Apis (whom it did not affect), and rode in to tell me.

It was obvious that a thinker of that bull's type would also be meticulous in his toilette; so, when he was sent to Arles, I warned our consignees to exercise caution with him. Happily, the change of scene, the music, the general attention, and the meeting again with old friends – all our bad boys attended – agreeably distracted him. He became for the time a pure *farceur* again; but his wheelings, his rushes, his rat-huntings were more superb than ever. There was in them now, you understand, a breadth of technique that comes of reasoned art, and, above all, the passion that arrives after experience. Oh, he had learned, out there on the Crau! At the end of his little turn, he was, according to local rules, to be handled in all respects except for the sword, which was a stick, as a professional bull who must die. He was manoeuvred into, or he posed himself in, the proper attitude; made his rush; received the point on his shoulder and then – turned about and cantered toward the door by which he had entered the arena. He said to the world: "My friends, the presentation is ended. I thank you for your applause. I go to repose myself." But our Arlesians, who are – not so clever as some, demanded an encore, and Apis was headed back again. We others from his country, we knew what would happen. He went to the centre of the ring, kneeled, and, slowly, with full parade, plunged his horns alternately in the dirt till the pads came off. Christophe shouts: "Leave him alone, you straight-nosed imbeciles! Leave him before you must." But they required emotion; for Rome has always debauched her loved Provincia with bread and circuses. It was given. Have you, Monsieur, ever seen a servant, with pan and broom, sweeping round the base-board of a room? In a half-minute Apis has them all swept out and over the barrier. Then he demands once more that the door shall be opened to him. It is opened and he retires as though – which, truly, is the case – loaded with laurels.'

Monsieur Voiron refilled the glasses, and allowed himself a cigarette, which he puffed for some time.

'And afterwards?' I said.

'I am arranging it in my mind. It is difficult to do it justice. Afterwards – yes, afterwards – Apis returned to his pastures and his mistresses and I to my business. I am no longer a scandalous old "sportif" in shirt-sleeves howling encouragement to the yellow son of a cow. I revert to Voiron Frères – wines, chemical manures, *et cetera*. And next year, through some chicane which I have not the leisure to unravel, and also, thanks to our patriarchal system of paying our older men out of the increase of the herds, old Christophe possesses himself of Apis. Oh, yes, he proves it through descent from a certain cow that my father had given his father before the Republic. Beware, Monsieur, of the memory of the illiterate man! An ancestor of Christophe had been a soldier under our Soult against your Beresford, near Bayonne. He fell into the hands of Spanish guerrillas. Christophe and his wife used to tell me the details on certain Saints' Days when I was a child. Now, as compared with our recent war, Soult's campaign and retreat across the Bidassoa –'

'But did you allow Christophe just to annex the bull?' I demanded.

'You do not know Christophe. He had sold him to the Spaniards before he informed me. The Spaniards pay in coin – douros of very pure silver. Our peasants mistrust our paper. You know the saying: "A thousand francs paper; eight hundred metal, and the cow is yours." Yes, Christophe sold Apis, who was then two and a half years old, and to Christophe's knowledge thrice at least an assassin.'

'How was that?' I said.

'Oh, his own kind only; and always, Christophe told me, by the same oblique rush from behind, the same sideways overthrow, and the same swift disembowelment, followed by this levitical cleaning of the horns. In human life he would have kept a manicurist – this Minotaur. And so, Apis disappears from our country. That does not trouble me. I know in due time I shall be advised. Why? Because, in this land, Monsieur, not a hoof moves between Berre and the Saintes Maries without the knowledge of specialists such as Christophe. The beasts are the substance and the drama of their lives to them. So when Christophe tells me, a little before Easter Sunday, that Apis makes his début in the bull-ring of a small Catalan town on the road to Barcelona, it is only to pack my car and trundle there across the frontier with him. The place lacked importance and manufactures, but it had produced a matador of some reputation, who was condescending to show his art in his native town. They were even running one special train to the place. Now our French railway system is only execrable, but the Spanish – '

'You went down by road, didn't you?' said I.

'Naturally. It was not too good. Villamarti was the matador's name. He proposed to kill two bulls for the honour of his birthplace. Apis, Christophe told me, would be his second. It was an interesting trip, and that little city by the sea was ravishing. Their bull-ring dates from the middle of the seventeenth century. It is full of feeling. The ceremonial too – when the horsemen enter and ask the Mayor in his box to throw down the keys of the bull-ring – that was exquisitely conceived. You know, if the keys are caught in the horseman's hat, it is considered a good omen. They were perfectly caught. Our seats were in the front row beside the gates where the bulls enter, so we saw everything.

Villamarti's first bull was not too badly killed. The second matador, whose name escapes me, killed his without distinction – a foil to Villamarti. And the third, Chisto, a laborious, middle-aged professional who had never risen beyond a certain dull competence, was equally of the background. Oh, they are as jealous as the girls of the Comédie Française, these matadors! Villamarti's troupe stood ready for his second bull. The gates opened, and we saw Apis, beautifully balanced on his feet, peer coquettishly round the corner, as though he were at home. A picador – a mounted man with the long lance-goad – stood near the barrier on his right. He had not even troubled to turn his horse, for the capeadors – the men with the cloaks – were advancing to play Apis – to feel his psychology and intentions, according to the rules that are made for bulls who do not think . . . I did not realise the murder before it was accomplished! The wheel, the rush, the oblique charge from behind, the fall of horse and man were simultaneous. Apis leaped the horse, with whom he had no quarrel, and alighted, all four feet together (it was enough), between the man's shoulders, changed his beautiful feet on the carcass, and was away, pretending to fall nearly on his nose. Do you follow me? In that instant, by that stumble, he produced the impression that his adorable assassination was a mere bestial blunder. Then, Monsieur, I began to comprehend that it was an artist we had to deal with. He did not stand over the body to draw the rest of the troupe. He chose to reserve that trick. He let the attendants bear out the dead, and went on to amuse himself among the capeadors. Now to Apis, trained among our children in the yards, the cloak was simply a guide to the boy behind it. He pursued, you understand, the person, not the propaganda – the proprietor, not the journal. If a third of our electors of France were as wise, my friend! . . . But it was done leisurely, with humour and a touch of truculence. He romped after one man's cloak as a clumsy dog might do, but I observed that he kept the man on his terrible left side. Christophe whispered to me: "Wait for his mother's kick. When he has made the fellow confident it will arrive." It arrived in the middle of a gambol. My God! He lashed out in the air as he frisked. The man dropped like a sack, lifted one hand a little towards his head, and – that was all. So you see, a body was again at his disposition; a second time the cloaks ran up to draw him off, but, a second time, Apis refused his grand scene. A second time he acted that his murder was accident and – he convinced his audience! It was as though he had knocked over a bridge-gate in the marshes by mistake. Unbelievable? I saw it.'

The memory sent Monsieur Voiron again to the champagne, and I accompanied him.

'But Apis was not the sole artist present. They say Villamarti comes of a family of actors. I saw him regard Apis with a new eye. He, too, began to understand. He took his cloak and moved out to play him before they should bring on another picador. He had his reputation. Perhaps Apis knew it. Perhaps Villamarti reminded him of some boy with whom he has practised at home. At any rate Apis permitted it – up to a certain point; but he did not allow Villamarti the stage. He cramped him throughout. He dived and plunged clumsily and slowly, but always with menace and always closing in. We could see that the man was conforming to the bull – not the bull to the man; for Apis was playing him towards the centre of the ring, and, in a little while – I watched his face – Villamarti knew it. But I could not fathom the creature's motive. "Wait," said old Christophe. "He wants that picador on the white horse yonder. When he reaches his proper distance he will get him. Villamarti is his cover. He used me once that way." And so it was, my friend! With the clang of one of our own Seventy-fives, Apis dismissed Villamarti with his chest – breasted him over – and had arrived at his objective near the barrier. The same oblique charge; the head carried low for the sweep of the horns; the immense sideways fall of the horse, broken-legged and half-paralysed; the senseless man on the ground, and – behold Apis between them, backed against the barrier – his right covered by the horse; his left by the body of the man at his feet. The simplicity of it! Lacking the carts and tractors of his early parade-grounds he, being a genius, had extemporised with the materials at hand, and dug himself in. The troupe closed again, their left wing broken by the kicking horse, their right immobilised by the man's body which Apis bestrode with significance. Villamarti almost threw himself between the horns, but – it was more an appeal than an attack. Apis refused him. He held his base. A picador was sent at him – necessarily from the front, which alone was open. Apis charged – he who, till then, you realise, had not used the horn! The horse went over backwards, the man half beneath him. Apis halted, hooked him under the heart, and threw him to the barrier. We heard his head crack, but he was dead before he hit the wood. There was no demonstration from the audience. They, also, had begun to realise this Foch among bulls! The arena occupied itself again with the dead. Two of the troupe irresolutely tried to play him – God knows in what hope! – but he moved out to the centre of the ring. "Look!" said Christophe. "Now he goes to clean himself. That always frightened me." He knelt down; he began to clean his horns. The earth was hard. He worried at it in an ecstasy of absorption. As he laid his head along and rattled his ears, it was as though he were interrogating the Devils themselves upon their secrets, and always saying impatiently: "Yes, I know that – and *that* – and *that*! Tell me more – *more*!" In the silence that covered us, a woman cried: "He digs a grave! Oh, Saints, he digs a grave!" Some others echoed this – not loudly – as a wave echoes in a grotto of the sea.

And when his horns were cleaned, he rose up and studied poor Villamarti's troupe, eyes in eyes, one by one, with the gravity of an equal in intellect and the remote and merciless resolution of a master in his art. This was more terrifying than his toilette.'

'And they – Villamarti's men?' I asked.

'Like the audience, were dominated. They had ceased to posture, or stamp, or address insults to him. They conformed to him. The two other matadors stared. Only Chisto, the oldest, broke silence with some call or other, and Apis turned his head towards him. Otherwise he was isolated, immobile – sombre – meditating on those at his mercy. Ah!

'For some reason the trumpet sounded for the *banderilleras* – those gay hooked darts that are planted in the shoulders of bulls who do not think, after their neck-muscles are tired by lifting horses. When such bulls feel the pain, they check for an instant, and, in that instant, the men step gracefully aside. Villamarti's banderillero answered the trumpet mechanically – like one condemned. He stood out, poised the darts and stammered the usual patter of invitation . . . And after? I do not assert that Apis shrugged his shoulders, but he reduced the episode to its lowest elements, as could only a bull of Gaul. With his truculence was mingled always – owing to the shortness of his tail – a certain Rabelaisian abandon, especially when viewed from the rear. Christophe had often commented upon it. Now, Apis brought that quality into play. He circulated round that boy, forcing him to break up his beautiful poses. He studied him from various angles, like an incompetent photographer. He presented to him every portion of his anatomy except his shoulders. At intervals he feigned to run in upon him. My God, he was cruel! But his motive was obvious. He was playing for a laugh from

should synchronise with the fracture of the human morale. It
was achieved. The boy turned and ran towards the barrier. Apis
was on him before the laugh ceased; passed him; headed him –
what do I say? – herded him off to the left, his horns beside and
a little in front of his chest: he did not intend him to escape
into a refuge. Some of the troupe would have closed in, but
Villamarti cried: "If he wants him he will take him. Stand!"
They stood. Whether the boy slipped or Apis nosed him over
I could not see. But he dropped, sobbing. Apis halted like a
car with four brakes, struck a pose, smelt him very completely
and turned away. It was dismissal more ignominious than
degradation at the head of one's battalion. The representation
was finished. Remained only for Apis to clear his stage of the
subordinate characters.

'Ah! His gesture then! He gave a dramatic start – this Cyrano
of the Camargue – as though he was aware of them for the
first time. He moved. All their beautiful breeches twinkled
for an instant along the top of the barrier. He held the stage
alone! But Christophe and I, we trembled! For, observe, he
had now involved himself in a stupendous drama of which he
only could supply the third act. And, except for an audience
on the razor-edge of emotion, he had exhausted his material.
Molière himself – we have forgotten, my friend, to drink to
the health of that great soul – might have been at a loss. And
Tragedy is but a step behind Failure. We could see the four or
five Civil Guards, who are sent always to keep order, fingering
the breeches of their rifles. They were but waiting a word from
the Mayor to fire on him, as they do some times at a bull who
leaps the barrier among the spectators. They would, of course,
have killed or wounded several people – but that would not
have saved Apis.'

Monsieur Voiron drowned the thought at once, and wiped
his beard.

'At that moment Fate – the Genius of France, if you will
– sent to assist in the incomparable finale, none other than
Chisto, the eldest, and I should have said (but never again
will I judge!) the least inspired of all; mediocrity itself but,
at heart – and it is the heart that conquers always, my friend

– at heart an artist. He descended stiffly into the arena, alone and assured. Apis regarded him, his eyes in his eyes. The man took stance, with his cloak, and called to the bull as to an equal: "Now, Señor, we will show these honourable caballeros something together." He advanced thus against this thinker who at a plunge – a kick – a thrust – could, we all knew, have extinguished him. My dear friend, I wish I could convey to you something of the unaffected bonhomie, the humour, the delicacy, the consideration bordering on respect even, with which Apis, the supreme artist, responded to this invitation. It was the Master, wearied after a strenuous hour in the atelier, unbuttoned and at ease with some not inexpert but limited disciple. The telepathy was instantaneous between them. And for good reason! Christophe said to me: "All's well. That Chisto began among the bulls. I was sure of it when I heard him call just now. He has been a herdsman. He'll pull it off." There was a little feeling and adjustment, at first, for mutual distances and allowances.

'Oh, yes! And here occurred a gross impertinence of Villamarti. He had, after an interval, followed Chisto – to retrieve his reputation. My Faith! I can conceive the elder Dumas slamming his door on an intruder precisely as Apis did. He raced Villamarti into the nearest refuge at once. He stamped his feet outside it, and he snorted: "Go! I am engaged with an artist." Villamarti went – his reputation left behind for ever.

'Apis returned to Chisto saying: "Forgive the interruption. I am not always master of my time, but you were about to observe, my dear confrère . . . ?" Then the play began. Out of compliment to Chisto, Apis chose as his objective (every bull varies in this respect) the inner edge of the cloak – that nearest to the man's body. This allows but a few millimetres clearance in charging. But Apis trusted himself as Chisto trusted him, and, this time, he conformed to the man, with inimitable judgment and temper. He allowed himself to be played into the shadow or the sun, as the delighted audience demanded. He raged enormously; he feigned defeat; he despaired in statuesque abandon, and thence flashed into fresh paroxysms

of wrath – but always with the detachment of the true artist
who knows he is but the vessel of an emotion whence others,
not he, must drink. And never once did he forget that honest
Chisto's cloak was to him the gauge by which to spare even a
hair on the skin. He inspired Chisto too. My God! His youth
returned to that meritorious beef-sticker – the desire, the grace,
and the beauty of his early dreams. One could almost see that
girl of the past for whom he was rising, rising to these present
heights of skill and daring. It was his hour too – a miraculous
hour of dawn returned to gild the sunset. All he knew was
at Apis' disposition. Apis acknowledged it with all that he
had learned at home, at Arles and in his lonely murders on
our grazing-grounds. He flowed round Chisto like a river of
death – round his knees, leaping at his shoulders, kicking just
clear of one side or the other of his head; behind his back
hissing as he shaved by; and once or twice – inimitable! – he
reared wholly up before him while Chisto slipped back from
beneath the avalanche of that instructed body. Those two, my
dear friend, held five thousand people dumb with no sound
but of their breathings – regular as pumps. It was unbearable.
Beast and man realised together that we needed a change of
note – a *détente*. They relaxed to pure buffoonery. Chisto fell
back and talked to him outrageously. Apis pretended he had
never heard such language. The audience howled with delight.
Chisto slapped him; he took liberties with his short tail, to the
end of which he clung while Apis pirouetted; he played about
him in all postures; he had become the herdsman again – gross,
careless, brutal, but comprehending. Yet Apis was always the
more consummate clown. All that time (Christophe and I saw
it) Apis drew off towards the gates of the *toril* where so many
bulls enter but – have you ever heard of one that returned?
We knew that Apis knew that as he had saved Chisto, so
Chisto would save him. Life is sweet to us all; to the artist
who lives many lives in one, sweetest. Chisto did not fail
him. At the last, when none could laugh any longer, the
man threw his cape across the bull's back, his arm round his
neck. He flung up a hand at the gate, as Villamarti, young
and commanding, but *not* a herdsman, might have raised it,

and he cried: "Gentlemen, open to me and my honourable little donkey." They opened – I have misjudged Spaniards in my time! – those gates opened to the man and the bull together, and closed behind them. And then? From the Mayor to the Guardia Civil they went mad for five minutes, till the trumpets blew and the fifth bull rushed out – an unthinking black Andalusian. I suppose some one killed him. My friend, my very dear friend, to whom I have opened my heart, I confess that I did not watch. Christophe and I, we were weeping together like children of the same Mother. Shall we drink to Her?'

FICTION

I am sure that to-morrow every member of my craft will be grateful, Lord Balfour, that in your many-sided career you have never thought to compete in the ranks of professed workers in fiction.

As regards the subject, not the treatment, of Lord Balfour's speech, I think we may take it, gentlemen, that the evening light is much the same for all men. When the shadows lengthen one contrasts what one had intended to do in the beginning with what one has accomplished. That the experience is universal does not make it any less acid – especially when, as in my case, one has been extravagantly rewarded for having done what one could not have helped doing.

But recognition by one's equals and betters in one's own craft is a reward of which a man may be unashamedly proud – as proud as I am of the honour that comes to me to-night from your hands. For I know with whom you have seen fit to brigade me in the ranks of Literature. The fiction that I am worthy of that honour be upon your heads!

Yet, at least, the art that I follow is not an unworthy one. For Fiction is Truth's elder sister. Obviously. No one in the world knew what truth was till someone had told a story. So it is the oldest of the arts, the mother of history, biography, philosophy dogmatic (or doubtful, Lord Balfour), and, of course, of politics.

Fiction began when some man invented a story about another man. It developed when another man told tales about a woman. This strenuous epoch begat the first school of destructive criticism, as well as the First Critic, who spent his short but vivid life in trying to explain that a man need not be a hen to judge the merits of an omelette. He died; but the question he raised is still at issue. It was inherited by the earliest writers from their unlettered ancestors, who also bequeathed to them the entire stock of primeval plots and situations – those fifty ultimate comedies and tragedies to which the Gods mercifully limit human action and suffering.

This changeless aggregate of material workers in fiction through the ages have run into fresh moulds, adorned and adapted to suit the facts and the fancies of their own generation. The Elizabethans, for instance, stood on the edge of a new and wonderful world filled with happy possibilities. Their descendants, 350 years later, have been shot into a world as new and as wonderful, but not quite as happy. And in both ages you can see writers raking the dumps of the English language for words that shall range farther, hit harder, and explode over a wider area than the service-pattern words in common use.

This merciless search, trial, and scrapping of material is one with the continuity of life which, we all know, is as a tale that is told, and which writers feel should be well told. All men are interested in the reflection of themselves and their surroundings, whether in the pure heart of a crystal or in a muddy pool; and nearly every writer who supplies a reflection secretly desires a share of immortality for the pains he has been at in holding up the mirror – which also reflects himself. He may win his desire. Quite a dozen writers have achieved immortality in the past 2500 years. From a bookmaker's – a real bookmaker's – point of view the odds are not attractive, but Fiction is built on fiction. That is where it differs from the other Arts.

Most of the Arts admit the truth that it is not expedient to tell everyone everything. Fiction recognises no such bar. There is no human emotion or mood which it is forbidden to assault – there is no canon of reserve or pity that need be respected – in fiction. Why should there be? The man, after all, is not telling the truth. He is only writing fiction. While he writes it, his world will extract from it just so much of truth or pleasure as it requires for the moment. In time a little more, or much less, of the residue may be carried forward to the general account, and there, perhaps, diverted to ends of which the writer never dreamed.

Take a well-known instance. A man of overwhelming intellect and power goes scourged through life between the dread of insanity and the wrath of his own soul warring with a brutal age. He exhausts mind, heart, and brain in that battle: he consumes himself, and perishes in utter desolation. Out of all his agony remains one little book, his dreadful testament against his fellow-kind, which to-day serves as a pleasant tale for the young under the title of *Gulliver's Travels*. That, and a faint recollection of some baby-talk in some love-letters, is as much as the world has chosen to retain of Jonathan Swift, Master of Irony. Think of it! It is like tuning-down the glare of a volcano to light a child to bed!

The true nature and intention, then, of a writer's work does not lie within his own knowledge. And we know that the world makes little allowance for any glory of workmanship which a writer spends on material that does not interest. So it would seem that Fiction is one of the few "unsheltered" occupations, in that there is equal victimisation on both sides, and no connection between the writer's standard of life, his output, or his wages.

Under these conditions has grown up in England a literature lavish in all aspects – lavish with the inveterate unthrift of the English, who are never happy unless they are throwing things away. By virtue of that same weakness, or strength, it overlaps so sumptuously that one could abstract and bestow from the mere wastage of any literary age since Chaucer's enough of abundance and enjoyment to quicken half a world. Those who study in the treasure-houses of its past know what unregarded perfection of workmanship and what serene independence of design often went to fabricate the least among those treasures. And they know, also, the insolence of the greatest Masters, who were too pressed to wait on perfection in their haste to reveal to us some supreme jewel scarcely cleansed from the matrix. Our English literature, I think, has always been the expression of a race more anxious to deliver what was laid upon it than to measure the means and methods of delivery.

And this immense and profligate range of experience, invention, and passion is our incommunicable inheritance, which is drawn upon at every need, for multitudes who, largely, neither know nor care whence their need is met.

In every age some men gain temporary favour because they happen to have met a temporary need of their age. Yet, as regards their future, they stand on a perfect equality with their fellow-craftsmen. It is not permitted to any generation to know what, or how much, of its effort will be carried forward to the honour and grace of our literature. The utmost a writer can hope is that there may survive of his work a fraction good enough to be drawn upon later, to uphold or to embellish some ancient truth restated, or some old delight reborn.

Admitting this, a man may, by the exercise of a little imagination, persuade himself that he has acquired merit in his lifetime. Or, if imagination be lacking, he may be led to that comfortable conclusion by the magic of his own art heard as we have heard it from Lord Balfour to-night, on the lips of a man wise in life, and a Master not ignorant of the power of words.

THE SURVIVAL

Horace, Ode 22, Bk. V

SECURELY, after days
  Unnumbered, I behold
Kings mourn that promised praise
  Their cheating bards foretold.

Of earth-constricting wars,
  Of Princes passed in chains,
Of deeds out-shining stars,
  No word or voice remains.

Yet furthest times receive
  And to fresh praise restore,
Mere flutes that breathe at eve,
  Mere seaweed on the shore.

A smoke of sacrifice;
  A chosen myrtle-wreath;
An harlot's altered eyes;
  A rage 'gainst love or death;

Glazed snow beneath the moon;
  The surge of storm-bowed trees –
The Caesars perished soon,
  And Rome Herself: But these

Endure while Empires fall
  And Gods for Gods make room . . .
Which greater God than all
  Imposed the amazing doom?

A LEGEND OF TRUTH

ONCE on a time, the ancient legends tell,
Truth, rising from the bottom of her well,
Looked on the world, but, hearing how it lied,
Returned to her seclusion horrified.
There she abode, so conscious of her worth,
Not even Pilate's Question called her forth,
Nor Galileo, kneeling to deny
The Laws that hold our Planet 'neath the sky.
Meantime, her kindlier sister, whom men call
Fiction, did all her work and more than all,
With so much zeal, devotion, tact, and care,
That no one noticed Truth was otherwhere.

Then came a War when, bombed and gassed and mined,
Truth rose once more, perforce, to meet mankind,
And through the dust and glare and wreck of things,
Beheld a phantom on unbalanced wings,
Reeling and groping, dazed, dishevelled, dumb,
But semaphoring direr deeds to come.
Truth hailed and bade her stand; the quavering shade,
Clung to her knees and babbled, 'Sister, aid!
I am – I was – thy Deputy, and men
Besought me for my useful tongue or pen
To gloss their gentle deeds, and I complied,
And they, and thy demands, were satisfied.
But this – ' she pointed o'er the blistered plain,
Where men as Gods and devils wrought amain –
'This is beyond me! Take thy work again.'

Tables and pen transferred, she fled afar,
And Truth assumed the record of the War . . .
She saw, she heard, she read, she tried to tell
Facts beyond precedent and parallel –
Unfit to hint or breathe, much less to write,
But happening every minute, day and night.
She called for proof. It came. The dossiers grew.
She marked them, first, 'Return. This can't be true.'
Then, underneath the cold official word:
'This is not really half of what occurred.'

She faced herself at last, the story runs,
And telegraphed her sister: 'Come at once.
Facts out of hand. Unable overtake
Without your aid. Come back for Truth's own sake!
Co-equal rank and powers if you agree.
They need us both, but you far more than me!'

DAYSPRING MISHANDLED

C'est moi, c'est moi, c'est moi!
  Je suis la Mandragore!
La fille des beaux jours qui s'éveille à l'aurore –
  Et qui chante pour toi!

C. Nodier

IN the days beyond compare and before the Judgments, a genius called Graydon foresaw that the advance of education and the standard of living would submerge all mind-marks in one mudrush of standardised reading-matter, and so created the Fictional Supply Syndicate to meet the demand.

Since a few days' work for him brought them more money than a week's elsewhere, he drew many young men – some now eminent – into his employ. He bade them keep their eyes on the Sixpenny Dream Book, the Army and Navy Stores Catalogue (this for backgrounds and furniture as they changed), and *The Hearthstone Friend*, a weekly publication which specialised unrivalledly in the domestic emotions. Yet, even so, youth would not be denied, and some of the collaborated love-talk in 'Passion Hath Peril', and 'Ena's Lost Lovers', and the account of the murder of the Earl in 'The Wickwire Tragedies' – to name but a few masterpieces now never mentioned for fear of blackmail – was as good as anything to which their authors signed their real names in more distinguished years.

Among the young ravens driven to roost awhile on Graydon's ark was James Andrew Manallace – a darkish, slow northerner of the type that does not ignite, but must be detonated. Given written or verbal outlines of a plot, he was useless; but, with a half-dozen pictures round which to write his tale, he could astonish.

And he adored that woman who afterwards became the mother of Vidal Benzaquen,[1] and who suffered and died because she loved one unworthy. There was, also, among the company a mannered, bellied person called Alured Castorley, who talked and wrote about 'Bohemia', but was always afraid of being 'compromised' by the weekly suppers at Neminaka's Café in Hestern Square, where the Syndicate work was apportioned, and where everyone looked out for himself. He, too, for a time, had loved Vidal's mother, in his own way.

Now, one Saturday at Neminaka's, Graydon, who had given Manallace a sheaf of prints – torn from an extinct children's book called *Philippa's Queen* – on which to improvise, asked for results. Manallace went down into his ulster-pocket, hesitated for a moment, and said the stuff had turned into poetry on his hands.

'Bosh!'

'That's what it isn't,' the boy retorted. 'It's rather good.'

'Then it's no use to us.' Graydon laughed. 'Have you brought back the cuts?'

Manallace handed them over. There was a castle in the series; a knight or so in armour; an old lady in a horned head-dress; a young ditto; a very obvious Hebrew; a clerk, with pen and inkhorn, checking wine-barrels on a wharf; and a Crusader. On the back of one of the prints was a note, 'If he doesn't want to go, why can't he be captured and held to ransom?' Graydon asked what it all meant.

'I don't know yet. A comic opera, perhaps,' said Manallace.

Graydon, who seldom wasted time, passed the cuts on to someone else, and advanced Manallace a couple of sovereigns to carry on with, as usual; at which Castorley was angry and would have said something unpleasant but was suppressed. Half-way through supper, Castorley told the company that a relative had died and left him an independence; and that he now withdrew from 'hackwork' to follow 'Literature'. Generally, the Syndicate rejoiced in a comrade's good fortune, but Castorley had gifts of waking dislike. So the news was received with a vote of thanks,

---

[1] 'The Village that voted the Earth was Flat.' *A Diversity of Creatures.*

and he went out before the end, and, it was said, proposed to 'Dal Benzaquen's mother, who refused him. He did not come back. Manallace, who had arrived a little exalted, got so drunk before midnight that a man had to stay and see him home. But liquor never touched him above the belt, and when he had slept awhile, he recited to the gas-chandelier the poetry he had made out of the pictures; said that, on second thoughts, he would convert it into comic opera; deplored the Upas-tree influence of Gilbert and Sullivan; sang somewhat to illustrate his point; and – after words, by the way, with a negress in yellow satin – was steered to his rooms.

In the course of a few years, Graydon's foresight and genius were rewarded. The public began to read and reason upon higher planes, and the Syndicate grew rich. Later still, people demanded of their printed matter what they expected in their clothing and furniture. So, precisely as the three guinea hand-bag is followed in three weeks by its thirteen and seven-pence ha'penny, indistinguishable sister, they enjoyed perfect synthetic substitutes for Plot, Sentiment, and Emotion. Graydon died before the Cinema-caption school came in, but he left his widow twenty-seven thousand pounds.

Manallace made a reputation, and, more important, money for Vidal's mother when her husband ran away and the first symptoms of her paralysis showed. His line was the jocundly-sentimental Wardour Street brand of adventure, told in a style that exactly met, but never exceeded, every expectation.

As he once said when urged to 'write a real book': 'I've got my label, and I'm not going to chew it off. If you save people thinking, you can do anything with 'em.' His output apart, he was genuinely a man of letters. He rented a small cottage in the country and economised on everything, except the care and charges of Vidal's mother.

Castorley flew higher. When his legacy freed him from 'hackwork', he became first a critic – in which calling he loyally scalped all his old associates as they came up – and then looked for some speciality. Having found it (Chaucer was the prey), he consolidated his position before he occupied it, by his careful speech, his cultivated bearing, and the whispered words of his friends whom he, too, had saved the trouble of thinking. It followed that, when he published his first serious articles on Chaucer, all the world which is interested in Chaucer said: 'This is an authority.' But he was no impostor. He learned and knew his poet and his age; and in a month-long dog-fight in an austere literary weekly, met and mangled a recognised Chaucer expert of the day. He also, 'for old sakes' sake', as he wrote to a friend, went out of his way to review one of Manallace's books with an intimacy of unclean deduction (this was before the days of Freud) which long stood as a record. Some member of the extinct Syndicate took occasion to ask him if he would – for old sake's sake – help Vidal's mother to a new treatment. He answered that he had 'known the lady very slightly and the calls on his purse were so heavy that', etc. The writer showed the letter to Manallace, who said he was glad Castorley hadn't interfered. Vidal's mother was then wholly paralysed. Only her eyes could move, and those always looked for the husband who had left her. She died thus in Manallace's arms in April of the first year of the War.

During the War he and Castorley worked as some sort of departmental dishwashers in the Office of Co-ordinated Supervisals. Here Manallace came to know Castorley again. Castorley, having a sweet tooth, cadged lumps of sugar for his tea from a typist, and when she took to giving them to a younger man, arranged that she should be reported for smoking in unauthorised apartments. Manallace possessed himself of every detail of the affair, as compensation for the review of his book. Then there came a night when waiting for a big air-raid, the two men had talked humanly, and Manallace spoke of Vidal's mother. Castorley said something in reply, and from that hour – as was learned several years later – Manallace's real life-work and interests began.

The War over, Castorley set about to make himself Supreme Pontiff on Chaucer by methods not far removed from the employment of poison-gas. The English Pope was silent, through private griefs, and influenza had carried off the learned Hun who claimed continental allegiance. Thus Castorley crowed unchallenged from Upsala to Seville, while Manallace went back to his cottage with the photo of Vidal's mother over the mantelpiece. She seemed to have emptied out his life, and left him only fleeting interests in trifles. His private diversions were experiments of uncertain outcome, which, he said, rested him after a day's gadzooking and vitalstapping. I found him, for instance, one week-end, in his toolshed-scullery, boiling a brew of slimy barks which were, if mixed with oak-galls, vitriol and wine, to become an ink-powder. We boiled it till the Monday, and it turned into an adhesive stronger than birdlime, and entangled us both.

At other times, he would carry me off, once in a few weeks to sit at Castorley's feet, and hear him talk about Chaucer. Castorley's voice, bad enough in youth, when it could be shouted down, had, with culture and tact, grown almost insupportable. His mannerisms, too, had multiplied and set. He minced and mouthed, postured and chewed his words throughout those terrible evenings; and poisoned not only Chaucer, but every shred of English literature which he used to embellish him. He was shameless, too, as regarded self-advertisement and 'recognition' – weaving elaborate intrigues; forming petty friendships and confederacies, to be dissolved next week in favour of more promising alliances; fawning, snubbing, lecturing, organising and lying as unrestingly as a politician, in chase of the Knighthood due not to him (he always called on his Maker to forbid such a thought) but as tribute to Chaucer. Yet, sometimes, he could break from his obsession and prove how a man's work will try to save the soul of him. He would tell us charmingly of copyists of the fifteenth century in England and the Low Countries, who had multiplied the Chaucer MSS, of which there remained – he gave us the exact number – and how each scribe could by him (and, he implied, by him alone) be distinguished from every other by some peculiarity of letter-information, spacing or like trick of pen-work; and how he could fix the dates of their work within five years. Sometimes he would give us an hour of really interesting stuff and then return to his overdue 'recognition'. The changes sickened me, but Manallace defended him, as a master in his own line who had revealed Chaucer to at least one grateful soul.

This, as far as I remembered, was the autumn when Manallace holidayed in the Shetlands or the Faroes, and came back with a stone 'quern' – a hand corn-grinder. He said it interested him from the ethnological standpoint. His whim lasted till next harvest, and was followed by a religious spasm which, naturally, translated itself into literature. He showed me a battered and mutilated Vulgate of 1485, patched up the back with bits of legal parchments, which he had bought for thirty five shillings. Some monk's attempt to rubricate chapter-initials had caught, it seemed, his forlorn fancy, and he dabbled in shells of gold and silver paint for weeks.

That also faded out, and he went to the Continent to get local colour for a love-story, about Alva and the Dutch, and the next year I saw practically nothing of him. This released me from seeing much of Castorley, but, at intervals, I would go there to dine with him, when his wife – an unappetising, ash-coloured woman – made no secret that his friends wearied her almost as much as he did. But at a later meeting, not long after Manallace had finished his Low Countries' novel, I found Castorley charged to bursting-point with triumph and high information hardly withheld. He confided to me that a time was at hand when great matters would be made plain, and 'recognition' would be inevitable. I assumed, naturally, that there was fresh scandal or heresy afoot in Chaucer circles, and kept my curiosity within bounds.

In time, New York cabled that a fragment of a hitherto unknown Canterbury Tale lay safe in the steel-walled vaults of the seven-million-dollar Sunnapia Collection. It was news on an international scale – the New World exultant - the Old deploring the 'burden of British taxation which drove such treasures, etc.', and the lighter-minded journals disporting themselves according to their publics; for 'our Dan', as one earnest Sunday editor observed, 'lies closer to the national heart than we wot of'. Common decency made me call on Castorley, who, to my surprise, had not yet descended into the arena. I found him, made young again by joy, deep in just-passed proofs.

Yes, he said, it was all true. He had, of course, been in it from the first. There had been found one hundred and seven new lines of Chaucer tacked on to an abridged end of *The Persone's Tale*, the whole the work of Abraham Mentzius, better known as Mentzel of Antwerp (1388-1438/9) – I might remember he had talked about him – whose distinguishing peculiarities were a certain Byzantine formation of his *g*'s, the use of a 'sickle-slanted' reed-pen, which cut into the vellum at certain letters; and, above all, a tendency to spell English words on Dutch lines, whereof the manuscript carried one convincing proof. For instance (he wrote it out for me), a girl praying against an undesired marriage, says:–

> 'Ah Jesu-Moder, pitie my oe peyne.
> Daiespringe mishandeelt cometh nat agayne.'

Would I, please, note the spelling of 'mishandeelt'? Stark Dutch and Mentzel's besetting sin! But in *his* position one took nothing for granted. The page had been part of the stiffening of the side of an old Bible, bought in a parcel by Dredd, the big dealer, because it had some rubricated chapter-initials, and by Dredd shipped, with a consignment of similar odds and ends, to the Sunnapia Collection, where they were making a glass-cased exhibit of the whole history of illumination and did not care how many books they gutted for that purpose. There, someone who noticed a crack in the back of the volume had unearthed it. He went on: 'They didn't know what to make of the thing at first. But they knew about *me*! They kept quiet till I'd been consulted. You might have noticed I was out of England for three months.

'I was over there, of course. It was what is called a "spoil" – a page Mentzel had spoiled with his Dutch spelling – I expect he had had the English dictated to him – then had evidently used the vellum for trying out his reeds; and then, I suppose, had put it away. The "spoil" had been doubled, pasted together, and slipped in as stiffening to the old book-cover. I had it steamed open, and analysed the wash. It gave the flour-grains in the paste – coarse, because of the old millstone – and there were traces of the grit itself. What? Oh, possibly a handmill of Mentzel's own time. He may have doubled the spoilt page and used it for part of a pad to steady wood-cuts on. It may have knocked about his

workshop for years. That, indeed, is practically certain because
a beginner from the Low Countries has tried his reed on a few
lines of some monkish hymn – not a bad lilt tho' – which must
have been common form. Oh yes, the page may have been used
in other books before it was used for the Vulgate. That doesn't
matter, but *this* does. Listen! I took a wash, for analysis, from a
blot in one corner – that would be after Mentzel had given up
trying to make a possible page of it, and had grown careless –
and I got the actual *ink* of the period! It's a practically eternal
stuff compounded on – I've forgotten his name for the minute
– the scribe at Bury St Edmunds, of course – hawthorn bark
and wine. Anyhow, on *his* formula. *That* wouldn't interest you
either, but, taken with all the other testimony, it clinches the
thing. (You'll see it all in my Statement to the Press on Monday.)
Overwhelming, isn't it?'

'Overwhelming,' I said, with sincerity. 'Tell me what the tale
was about, though. That's more in my line.'

'I know it; but *I* have to be equipped on all sides. The verses
are relatively easy for one to pronounce on. The freshness, the
fun, the humanity, the fragrance of it all, cries – no, shouts
– itself as Dan's work. Why "Daiespringe mishandled" alone
stamps it from Dan's mint. Plangent as doom, my dear boy -
plangent as doom! It's all in my Statement. Well, substantially,
the fragment deals with a girl whose parents wish her to marry
an elderly suitor. The mother isn't so keen on it, but the father,
an old Knight, is. The girl, of course, is in love with a younger
and a poorer man. Common form? Granted. Then the father,
who doesn't in the least want to, is ordered off to a Crusade
and, by way of passing on the kick, as we used to say during
the War, orders the girl to be kept in duress till his return or
her consent to the old suitor. Common form, again? Quite so.
That's too much for her mother. She reminds the old Knight
of his age and infirmities, and the discomforts of Crusading.
Are you sure I'm not boring you?'

'Not at all,' I said, though time had begun to whirl backward
through my brain to a red-velvet, pomatum-scented side-room
at Neminaka's and Manallace's set face intoning to the gas.

'You'll read it all in my Statement next week. The sum is

that the old lady tells him of a certain Knight-adventurer on the French coast, who, for a consideration, waylays Knights who don't relish crusading and holds them to impossible ransoms till the trooping-season is over, or they are returned sick. He keeps a ship in the Channel to pick 'em up and transfers his birds to his castle ashore, where he has a reputation for doing 'em well. As the old lady points out:

> 'And if perchance thou fall into his honde
> By God how canstow ride to Holilonde?'

'You see? Modern in essence as Gilbert and Sullivan, but handled as only Dan could! And she reminds him that "Honour and olde bones" parted company long ago. He makes one splendid appeal for the spirit of chivalry:

> Lat all men change as Fortune may send,
> But Knighthood beareth service to the end,

and *then*, of course, he gives in:

> For what his woman willeth to be don
> Her manne must or wauken Hell anon.

'Then she hints that the daughter's young lover, who is in the Bordeaux wine-trade, could open negotiations for a kidnapping without compromising him. And *then* that careless brute Mentzel spoils his page and chucks it! But there's enough to show what's going to happen. You'll see it all in my Statement. Was there ever anything in literary finds to hold a candle to it? . . . and they give grocers Knighthoods for selling cheese!'

I went away before he could get into his stride on that course. I wanted to think, and to see Manallace. But I waited till Castorley's Statement came out. He had left himself no loophole. And when, a little later, his (nominally the Sunnapia people's) 'scientific' account of their analyses and tests appeared, criticism ceased, and some journals began to demand 'public recognition'. Manallace wrote me on this subject, and I went down to his cottage, where he at once asked me to sign a Memorial on Castorley's behalf. With luck, he said, we might get him a KBE in the next Honours List. Had I read the Statement?

'I have,' I replied. 'But I want to ask you something first. Do you remember the night you got drunk at Neminaka's, and I stayed behind to look after you?'

'Oh, *that* time,' said he, pondering. 'Wait a minute! I remember Graydon advancing me two quid. He was a generous paymaster. And I remember – now, who the devil rolled me under the sofa – and what for?'

'We all did,' I replied. 'You wanted to read us what you'd written to those Chaucer cuts.'

'I don't remember that. No! I don't remember anything after the sofa-episode . . . *You* always said that you took me home – didn't you?'

'I did, and you told Kentucky Kate outside the old Empire that you had been faithful, Cynara, in your fashion.'

'Did I?' said he. 'My God! Well, I suppose I have.' He stared into the fire. 'What else?'

'Before we left Neminaka's you recited me what you had made out of the cuts – the whole tale! So – you see?'

'Ye-es.' He nodded. 'What are you going to do about it?'

'What are *you*?'

'I'm going to help him get his Knighthood – first.'

'Why?'

'I'll tell you what he said about 'Dal's mother – the night there was that air-raid on the offices.'

He told it.

'That's why,' he said. 'Am I justified?'

He seemed to me entirely so.

'But after he gets his Knighthood?' I went on.

'That depends. There are several things I can think of. It interests me.'

'Good Heavens! I've always imagined you a man without interests.'

'So I was. I owe my interests to Castorley. He gave me every one of 'em except the tale itself.'

'How did *that* come?'

'Something in those ghastly cuts touched off something in me
– a sort of possession, I suppose. I was in love too. No wonder I got
drunk that night. I'd *been* Chaucer for a week! Then I thought
the notion might make a comic opera. But Gilbert and Sullivan
were too strong.'

'So I remember you told me at the time.'

'I kept it by me, and it made me interested in Chaucer –
philologically and so on. I worked on it on those lines for years.
There wasn't a flaw in the wording even in '14. I hardly had to
touch it after that.'

'Did you ever tell it to anyone except me?'

'No, only 'Dal's mother – when she could listen to anything –
to put her to sleep. But when Castorley said – what he did about
her, I thought I might use it. 'Twasn't difficult. *He* taught me.
D'you remember my birdlime experiments, and the stuff on
our hands? I'd been trying to get that ink for more than a year.
Castorley told me where I'd find the formula. And your falling
over the quern, too?'

'That accounted for the stone-dust under the microscope?'

'Yes. I grew the wheat in the garden here, and ground it
myself. Castorley gave me Mentzel complete. He put me on
to an MS in the British Museum which he said was the finest
sample of his work. I copied his "Byzantine *g*'s" for months.'

'And what's a "sickle-slanted" pen?' I asked.

'You nick one edge of your reed till it drags and scratches
on the curves of the letters. Castorley told me about Mentzel's
spacing and margining. I only had to get the hang of his script.'

'How long did that take you?'

'On and off – some years. I was too ambitious at first – I
wanted to give the whole poem. That would have been risky.
Then Castorley told me about spoiled pages and I took the hint.
I spelt "Dayspring mishandeelt" Mentzel's way – to make sure
of him. It's not a bad couplet in itself. Did you see how he
admires the "plangency" of it?'

'Never mind him. Go on!' I said.

He did. Castorley had been his unfailing guide throughout,
specifying in minutest detail every trap to be set later for his

own feet. The actual vellum was an Antwerp find, and its
introduction into the cover of the Vulgate was begun after
a long course of amateur bookbinding. At last, he bedded
it under pieces of an old deed, and a printed page (1686)
of Horace's *Odes*, legitimately used for repairs by different
owners in the seventeenth and eighteenth centuries; and at
the last moment, to meet Castorley's theory that spoiled pages
were used in workshops by beginners, he had written a few Latin
words in fifteenth century script – the Statement gave the exact
date – across an open part of the fragment. The thing ran: *'Illa
alma Mater ecca, secum afferens me acceptum. Nicolaus Atrib.'*
The disposal of the thing was easiest of all. He had merely hung
about Dredd's dark bookshop of fifteen rooms, where he was
well known, occasionally buying but generally browsing, till,
one day, Dredd Senior showed him a case of cheap black-letter
stuff, English and Continental – being packed for the Sunnapia
people – into which Manallace tucked his contribution, taking
care to wrench the back enough to give a lead to an earnest seeker.

'And then?' I demanded.

'After six months or so Castorley sent for me. Sunnapia had
found it, and as Dredd had missed it, and there was no money-
motive sticking out, they were half convinced it was genuine
from the start. But they invited him over. He conferred with
their experts, and suggested the scientific tests. *I* put that into
his head, before he sailed. That's all. And now, will you sign
our Memorial?'

I signed. Before we had finished hawking it round there was
a host of influential names to help us, as well as the impetus
of all the literary discussion which arose over every detail of the
glorious trove. The upshot was a KBE[1] for Castorley in the next
Honours List; and Lady Castorley, her cards duly printed, called
on friends that same afternoon.

Manallace invited me to come with him, a day or so later,
to convey our pleasure and satisfaction to them both. We were
rewarded by the sight of a man relaxed and ungirt – not to

---

[1] Officially it was on account of his good work in the Departmental of Co-ordinated
Supervisals, but all true lovers of literature knew the real reason, and told the papers
so.

say wallowing naked – on the crest of Success. He assured us that 'The Title' should not make any difference to our future relations, seeing it was in no sense personal, but, as he had often said, a tribute to Chaucer; 'and, after all,' he pointed out, with a glance at the mirror over the mantelpiece, 'Chaucer was the prototype of the "veray parfit gentil Knight" of the British Empire so far as that then existed.'

On the way back, Manallace told me he was considering either an unheralded revelation in the baser Press which should bring Castorley's reputation about his own ears some breakfast-time, or a private conversation, when he would make clear to Castorley that he must now back the forgery as long as he lived, under threat of Manallace's betraying it if he flinched.

He favoured the second plan. 'If I pull the string of the shower-bath in the papers,' he said, 'Castorley might go off his veray parfit gentil nut. I want to keep his intellect.'

'What about your own position? The forgery doesn't matter so much. But if you tell this you'll kill him,' I said.

'I intend that. Oh – my position? I've been dead since – April, Fourteen, it was. But there's no hurry. What was it *she* was saying to you just as we left?'

'She told me how much your sympathy and understanding had meant to him. She said she thought that even Sir Alured did not realise the full extent of his obligations to you.'

'She's right, but I don't like her putting it that way.'

'It's only common form – as Castorley's always saying.'

'Not with *her*. She can hear a man think.'

'She never struck me in that light.'

'*You* aren't playing against her.'

'Guilty conscience, Manallace?'

'H'm! I wonder. Mine or hers? I *wish* she hadn't said that. "More even than *he* realises it." I won't call again for awhile.'

He kept away till we read that Sir Alured, owing to slight indisposition, had been unable to attend a dinner given in his honour.

Inquiries brought word that it was but natural reaction, after strain, which, for the moment, took the form of nervous dyspepsia, and he would be glad to see Manallace at any time.

Manallace reported him as rather pulled and drawn, but full of his new life and position, and proud that his efforts should have martyred him so much. He was going to collect, collate, and expand all his pronouncements and inferences into one authoritative volume.

'I must make an effort of my own,' said Manallace. 'I've collected nearly all his stuff about the Find that has appeared in the papers, and he's promised me everything that's missing. I'm going to help him. It will be a new interest.'

'How will you treat it?' I asked.

'I expect I shall quote his deductions on the evidence, and parallel 'em with my experiments – the ink and the paste and the rest of it. It ought to be rather interesting.'

'But even then there will only be your word. It's hard to catch up with an established lie,' I said. 'Especially when you've started it yourself.'

He laughed. 'I've arranged for *that* – in case anything happens to me. Do you remember the "Monkish Hymn"?'

'Oh yes! There's quite a literature about it already.'

'Well, you write those ten words above each other, and read down the first and second letters of 'em; and see what you get.[1] My Bank has the formula.'

He wrapped himself lovingly and leisurely round his new task, and Castorley was as good as his word in giving him help. The two practically collaborated, for Manallace suggested that all Castorley's strictly scientific evidence should be in one place, with his deductions and dithyrambs as appendices. He assured him that the public would prefer this arrangement, and, after grave consideration, Castorley agreed.

'That's better,' said Manallace to me. 'Now I sha'n't have

[1] *Illa*
alma
Mater
ecca
secum
afferens
me
acceptum
Nicolaus
Atrib.

so many hiatuses in my extracts. Dots always give the reader the idea you aren't dealing fairly with your man. I shall merely quote him solid, and rip him up, proof for proof, and date for date, in parallel columns. His book's taking more out of him than I like, though. He's been doubled up twice with tummy attacks since I've worked with him. And he's just the sort of flatulent beast who may go down with appendicitis.'

We learned before long that the attacks were due to gall-stones, which would necessitate an operation. Castorley bore the blow very well. He had full confidence in his surgeon, an old friend of theirs; great faith in his own constitution; a strong conviction that nothing would happen to him till the book was finished, and, above all, the Will to Live.

He dwelt on these assets with a voice at times a little out of pitch and eyes brighter than usual beside a slightly-sharpening nose.

I had only met Gleeag, the surgeon, once or twice at Castorley's house, but had always heard him spoken of as a most capable man. He told Castorley that his trouble was the price exacted, in some shape or other, from all who had served their country; and that, measured in units of strain, Castorley had practically been at the front through those three years he had served in the Office of Co-ordinated Supervisals. However, the thing had been taken betimes, and in a few weeks he would worry no more about it.

'But suppose he dies?' I suggested to Manallace.

'He won't. I've been talking to Gleeag. He says he's all right.'

'Wouldn't Gleeag's talk be common form?'

'I *wish* you hadn't said that. But, surely, Gleeag wouldn't have the face to play with me – or her.'

'Why not? I expect it's been done before.'

But Manallace insisted that, in this case, it would be impossible.

The operation was a success and, some weeks later, Castorley began to recast the arrangement and most of the material of his book. 'Let me have my way,' he said, when Manallace protested. 'They are making too much of a baby of me. I really don't need Gleeag looking in every day now.' But Lady Castorley told us that he required careful watching. His heart had felt the strain, and fret or disappointment of any kind must be avoided. 'Even,' she turned to Manallace, 'though you know ever so much better how his book should be arranged than he does himself.'

'But really,' Manallace began. 'I'm very careful not to fuss –'

She shook her finger at him playfully. 'You don't think you do; but, remember, he tells me everything that you tell him, just the same as he told me everything that he used to tell *you*. Oh, I don't mean the things that men talk about. I mean about his Chaucer.'

'I didn't realise that,' said Manallace, weakly.

'I thought you didn't. He never spares me anything; but *I* don't mind,' she replied with a laugh, and went off to Gleeag, who was paying his daily visit. Gleeag said he had no objection to Manallace working with Castorley on the book for a given time – say, twice a week – but supported Lady Castorley's demand that he should not be over-taxed in what she called 'the sacred hours'. The man grew more and more difficult to work with, and the little check he had heretofore set on his self-praise went altogether.

'He says there has never been anything in the History of Letters to compare with it,' Manallace groaned. 'He wants now to inscribe – he never dedicates, you know – inscribe it to me, as his "most valued assistant". The devil of it is that *she* backs him up in getting it out soon. Why? How much do you think she knows?'

'Why should she know anything at all?'

'You heard her say he had told her everything that he had told me about Chaucer? (I *wish* she hadn't said that!) If she puts two and two together, she can't help seeing that every one of his notions and theories has been played up to. But then – but then . . . Why is she trying to hurry publication? She talks about me fretting him. *She's* at him, all the time, to be quick.'

Castorley must have overworked, for, after a couple of months, he complained of a stitch in his right side, which Gleeag said was a slight sequel, a little incident of the operation. It threw him back awhile, but he returned to his work undefeated.

The book was due in the autumn. Summer was passing, and

his publisher urgent, and – he said to me, when after a longish interval I called – Manallace had chosen this time, of all, to take a holiday. He was not pleased with Manallace, once his indefatigable *aide*, but now dilatory, and full of time-wasting objections. Lady Castorley had noticed it, too.

Meantime, with Lady Castorley's help, he himself was doing the best he could to expedite the book; but Manallace had mislaid (did I think through jealousy?) some essential stuff which had been dictated to him. And Lady Castorley wrote Manallace, who had been delayed by a slight motor accident abroad, that the fret of waiting was prejudicial to her husband's health. Manallace, on his return from the Continent, showed me that letter.

'He has fretted a little, I believe,' I said.

Manallace shuddered. 'If I stay abroad, I'm helping to kill him. If I help him to hurry up the book, I'm expected to kill him. *She* knows,' he said.

'You're mad. You've got this thing on the brain.'

'I have not! Look here! You remember that Gleeag gave me from four to six, twice a week, to work with him. She called them the ''sacred hours''. You heard her? Well, they *are*! They are Gleeag's and hers. But she's so infernally plain, and I'm such a fool, it took me weeks to find it out.'

'That's their affair,' I answered. 'It doesn't prove she knows anything about the Chaucer.'

'She *does*! He told her everything that he had told me when I was pumping him, all those years. She put two and two together when the thing came out. She saw exactly how I had set my traps. I know it! She's been trying to make me admit it.'

'What did you do?

'Didn't understand what she was driving at, of course. And then she asked Gleeag, before me, if he didn't think the delay over the book was fretting Sir Alured. He didn't think so. He said getting it out might deprive him of an interest. He had that much decency. *She's* the devil!'

'What do you suppose is her game, then?'

'If Castorley knows he's been had, it'll kill him. She's at me all the time, indirectly, to let it out. I've told you she wants to make it a sort of joke between us. Gleeag's willing to wait. He knows Castorley's a dead man. It slips out when they talk. They say "He was", not "He is". Both of 'em know it. But *she* wants him finished sooner.'

'I don't believe it. What are you going to do?'

'What can I? I'm not going to have him killed, though.'

Manlike, he invented compromises whereby Castorley might be lured up by-paths of interest, to delay publication. This was not a success. As autumn advanced Castorley fretted more, and suffered from returns of his distressing colics. At last, Gleeag told him that he thought they might be due to an overlooked gallstone working down. A second comparatively trivial operation would eliminate the bother once and for all. If Castorley cared for another opinion, Gleeag named a surgeon of eminence. 'And then,' said he, cheerily, 'the two of us can talk you over.' He was oppressed by pains in his side, which, at first, had yielded to the liver-tonics Gleeag prescribed; but now they stayed – like a toothache – behind everything. He felt more at ease in his bedroom-study, with his proofs round him. If he had more pain than he could stand, he would consider the second operation. Meantime Manallace – 'the meticulous Manallace', he called him – agreed with him in thinking that the Mentzel page-facsimile, done by the Sunnapia Library, was not quite good enough for the great book, and the Sunnapia people were, very decently, having it re-processed. This would hold things back till early spring, which had its advantages for he could run a fresh eye over all in the interval.

One gathered these news in the course of stray visits as the days shortened. He insisted on Manallace keeping to the 'sacred hours', and Manallace insisted on my accompanying him when possible. On these occasions he and Castorley would confer apart for half an hour or so, while I listened to an unendurable clock in the drawing-room. Then I would join them and help wear out the rest of the time, while Castorley rambled. His speech, now, was often clouded and uncertain – the result of the 'liver-tonics'; and his face came to look like old vellum.

It was a few days after Christmas – the operation had been postponed till the following Friday – that we called together. She met us with word that Sir Alured had picked up an irritating little winter cough, due to a cold wave, but we were not, therefore, to abridge our visit. We found him in steam perfumed with Friar's Balsam. He waved the old Sunnapia facsimile at us. We agreed that it ought to have been more worthy. He took a dose of his mixture, lay back and asked us to lock the door. There was, he whispered, something wrong somewhere. He could not lay his finger on it, but it was in the air. He felt he was being played with. He did not like it. There was something wrong all round him. Had we noticed it? Manallace and I severally and slowly denied that we had noticed anything of the sort.

With no longer break than a light fit of coughing, he fell into the hideous, helpless panic of the sick – those worse than captives who lie at the judgment and mercy of the hale for every office and hope. He wanted to go away. Would we help him to pack his Gladstone? Or, if that would attract too much attention in certain quarters, help him to dress and go out? There was an urgent matter to be set right, and now that he had The Title and knew his own mind it would all end happily and he would be well again. *Please* would we let him go out, just to speak to – he named her; he named her by her 'little' name out of the old Neminaka days? Manallace quite agreed, and recommended a pull at the 'liver-tonic' to brace him after so long in the house. He took it, and Manallace suggested that it would be better if, after his walk, he came down to the cottage for a week-end and brought the revise with him. They could then re-touch the last chapter. He answered to that drug and to some praise of his work, and presently simpered drowsily. Yes, it *was* good – though he said it who should not. He praised himself awhile till, with a puzzled forehead and shut eyes, he told us that *she* had been saying lately that it was too good – the whole thing, if we understood, was *too* good. He wished us to get the exact shade of her meaning. She had suggested, or rather implied, this doubt. She had said – he would let us draw our own inferences – that the Chaucer find had 'anticipated the wants of humanity'. Johnson, of course. No need to tell *him* that. But what the hell was her implication? Oh God! Life had always been one long innuendo! *And* she had said that a man could do anything with anyone if he saved him the trouble of thinking. What did she mean by that? *He* had never shirked thought. He had thought sustainedly all his life. It *wasn't* too good, was it? Manallace didn't think it was too good – did he? But this pick-pick-picking at a man's brain and work was too bad, wasn't it? *What* did she mean? Why did she always bring in Manallace, who was only a friend – no scholar, but a lover of the game – Eh? – Manallace could confirm this if he were here, instead of loafing on the Continent just when he was most needed.

'I've come back,' Manallace interrupted, unsteadily. 'I can confirm every word you've said. You've nothing to worry about. It's *your* find – *your* credit – *your* glory and – all the rest of it.'

'Swear you'll tell her so then,' said Castorley. 'She doesn't believe a word I say. She told me she never has since before we were married. Promise!'

Manallace promised, and Castorley added that he had named him his literary executor, the proceeds of the book to go to his wife. 'All profits without deduction,' he gasped. 'Big sales if it's properly handled. *You* don't need money . . . Graydon'll trust *you* to any extent. It 'ud be a long . . .'

He coughed, and, as he caught breath, his pain broke through all the drugs, and the outcry filled the room. Manallace rose to fetch Gleeag, when a full, high, affected voice, unheard for a generation, accompanied, as it seemed, the clamour of a beast in agony, saying: 'I wish to God someone would stop that old swine howling down there! *I* can't . . . I was going to tell you fellows that it would be a dam' long time before Graydon advanced *me* two quid.'

We escaped together, and found Gleeag waiting, with Lady Castorley, on the landing. He telephoned me, next morning, that Castorley had died of bronchitis, which his weak state made it impossible for him to throw off. 'Perhaps it's just as well,' he added, in reply to the condolences I asked him to convey to the widow. 'We might have come across something we couldn't have coped with.'

Distance from that house made me bold.

'You knew all along, I suppose? What was it, really?'

'Malignant kidney-trouble – generalised at the end.' No use worrying him about it. We let him through as easily as possible. Yes! A happy release . . . What? . . . Oh! Cremation. Friday, at eleven.'

There, then, Manallace and I met. He told me that she had asked him whether the book need now be published; and he had told her this was more than ever necessary, in her interests as well as Castorley's.

'She is going to be known as his widow – for a while, at any rate. Did I perjure myself much with him?'

'Not explicitly,' I answered.

'Well, I have now – with *her* – explicitly,' said he, and took out his black gloves . . .

As, on the appointed words, the coffin crawled sideways through the noiselessly-closing door-flaps, I saw Lady Castorley's eyes turn towards Gleeag.

GERTRUDE'S PRAYER

(Modernised from the 'Chaucer' of Manallace.)

THAT which is marred at birth Time shall not mend,
    Nor water out of bitter well make clean;
All evil thing returneth at the end,
    Or elseway walketh in our blood unseen.
Whereby the more is sorrow in certaine –
Dayspring mishandled cometh not againe.

To-bruized be that slender, sterting spray
    Out of the oake's rind that should betide
A branch of girt and goodliness, straightway
    Her spring is turnèd on herself, and wried
And knotted like some gall or veiney wen. –
Dayspring mishandled cometh not agen.

Noontide repayeth never morning-bliss –
    Sith noon to morn is incomparable;
And, so it be our dawning goth amiss,
    None other after-hour serveth well.
Ah! Jesu-Moder, pitie my oe paine –
Dayspring mishandled cometh not againe!

'PROOFS OF HOLY WRIT'

Arise, shine; for thy light is come, and the glory of the Lord is risen upon thee.

2. For, behold, the darkness shall cover the earth, and gross darkness the people: but the Lord shall arise upon thee, and his glory shall be seen upon thee.

3. And the Gentiles shall come to thy light, and kings to the brightness of thy rising.

*   *   *   *   *

19. The sun shall be no more thy light by day; neither for brightness shall the moon give light unto thee: but the Lord shall be unto thee an everlasting light, and thy God thy glory.

20. Thy sun shall no more go down; neither shall thy moon withdraw itself: for the Lord shall be thine everlasting light, and the days of thy mourning shall be ended.

Isaiah lx. Authorised Version

THEY seated themselves in the heavy chairs on the pebbled floor beneath the eaves of the summerhouse by the orchard. A table between them carried wine and glasses, and a packet of papers, with pen and ink. The larger man of the two, his doublet unbuttoned, his broad face blotched and scarred, puffed a little as he came to rest. The other picked an apple from the grass, bit it, and went on with the thread of the talk that they must have carried out of doors with them.

'But why waste time fighting atomies who do not come up to your belly-button, Ben?' he asked.

'It breathes me – it breathes me, between bouts! *You*'d be better for a tussle or two.'

'But not to spend mind and verse on 'em. What was Dekker to you? Ye knew he'd strike back – and hard.'

'He and Marston had been baiting me like dogs . . . about my trade as they called it, though it was only my cursed stepfather's. "Bricks and mortar," Dekker said, and "hodman". And he mocked my face. 'Twas clean as curds in my youth. This humour has come on me since.'

'Ah! "Every man *and* his humour"? But why did ye not have at Dekker in peace – over the sack, as you do at me?'

'Because I'd have drawn on him – and he's no more worth a hanging than Gabriel. Setting aside what he wrote of me, too, the hireling dog has merit, of a sort. His *Shoemaker's Holiday*. Hey? Though my *Bartlemy Fair*, when 'tis presented, will furnish out three of it and – '

'Ride all the easier. I have suffered two readings of it already. It creaks like an overloaded hay-wain,' the other cut in. 'You give too much.'

Ben smiled loftily, and went on. 'But I'm glad I lashed him in my *Poetaster*, for all I've worked with him since. How comes it that I've never fought with thee, Will?'

'First, Behemoth,' the other drawled, 'it needs two to engender any sort of iniquity. Second, the betterment of this present age – and the next, maybe – lies, in chief, on our four shoulders. If the Pillars of the Temple fall out, Nature, Art, and Learning come to a stand. Last, I am not yet ass enough to hawk up my private spites before the groundlings. What do the Court, citizens, or 'prentices give for thy fallings-out or fallings-in with Dekker – or the Grand Devil?'

'They should be taught, then – taught.'

'Always *that*? What's your commission to enlighten us?'

'My own learning which I have heaped up, lifelong, at my own pains. My assured knowledge, also, of my craft and art. I'll suffer no man's mock or malice on it.'

'The one sure road to mockery.'

'I deny nothing of my brain-store to my lines. I – I build up my own works throughout.'

'Yet when Dekker cries "hodman" y'are not content.'

Ben half heaved in this chair. 'I'll owe you a beating for that when I'm thinner. Meantime, here's on account. I say, *I* build upon my own foundations; devising and perfecting my own plots; adorning 'em justly as fits time, place, and action. In all of which you sin damnably. *I* set no landward principalities on sea-beaches.'

'They pay their penny for pleasure – not learning,' Will answered above the apple-core.

'Penny or tester, you owe 'em justice. In the facture of plays – nay, listen, Will – at all points they must be dressed historically – *teres atque rotundus* – in ornament and temper. As my *Sejanus*, of which the mob was unworthy.'

Here Will made a doleful face, and echoed, 'Unworthy! I was – what did I play, Ben, in that long weariness? Some most grievous ass.'

'The part of Caius Silius,' said Ben stiffly.

Will laughed aloud. 'True. "Indeed that place *was* not my sphere." '

It must have been a quotation, for Ben winced a little, ere he recovered himself and went on: 'Also my *Alchemist* which the world in part apprehends. The main of its learning is necessarily yet hid from 'em. To come to your works, Will –'

'I am a sinner on all sides. The drink's at your elbow.'

'Confession shall not save ye – nor bribery.' Ben filled his glass. 'Sooner than labour the right cold heat to devise your own plots you filch, botch, and clap 'em together out o'ballads, broadsheets, old wives' tales, chap-books – '

Will nodded with complete satisfaction. 'Say on,' quoth he.

'"Tis so with nigh all yours. I've known honester jackdaws. And whom among the learned do ye deceive? Reckoning up those – forty, is it? – your plays you've misbegot, there's not six which have not plots common as Moorditch.'

'Ye're out, Ben. There's not one. My *Love's Labour* (how I came to write it, I know not) is nearest to lawful issue. My *Tempest* (how I came to write *that*, I know) is, in some part, my own stuff. Of the rest, I stand guilty. Bastards all!'

'And no shame?'

'None! Our business must be fitted with parts hot and hot

– and the boys are more trouble than the men. Give me the bones of any stuff, I'll cover 'em as quickly as any. But to hatch new plots is to waste God's unreturning time like a – ' – he chuckled – 'like a hen.'

'Yet see what ye miss! Invention next to Knowledge, whence it proceeds, being the chief glory of Art – '

'Miss, say you? Dick Burbage – in my *Hamlet* that I botched for him when he had staled of our Kings? (Nobly he played it.) Was *he* a miss?'

Ere Ben could speak Will overbore him.

'And when poor Dick was at odds with the world in general and womenkind in special, I clapped him up my *Lear* for a vomit.'

'An hotch-potch of passion, outrunning reason,' was the verdict.

'Not altogether. Cast in a mould too large for any boards to bear. (My fault!) Yet Dick evened it. And when he'd come out of his whoremongering aftermaths of repentance, I served him my *Macbeth* to toughen him. Was that a miss?'

'I grant you your *Macbeth* as nearest in spirit to my *Sejanus*; showing for example: "How fortune plies her sports when she begins To practise 'em." We'll see which of the two lives longest.'

'Amen! I'll bear no malice among the worms.'

A liveried serving-man, booted and spurred, led a saddle-horse through the gate into the orchard. At a sign from Will he tethered the beast to a tree, lurched aside and stretched on the grass. Ben, curious as a lizard, for all his bulk, wanted to know what it meant.

'There's a nosing Justice of the Peace lost in thee,' Will returned. 'Yon's a business I've neglected all this day for thy fat sake – and he by so much the drunker . . . Patience! It's all set out on the table. Have a care with the ink!'

Ben reached unsteadily for the packet of papers and read the superscription: ' "To William Shakespeare, Gentleman, at his house of New Place in the town of Stratford, these – with diligence from MS." Why does the fellow withhold his name? Or is it one of your women? I'll look?'

Muzzy as he was, he opened and unfolded a mass of printed papers expertly enough.

'From the most learned divine, Miles Smith of Brazen Nose College,' Will explained. 'You know this business as well as I. The King has set all the scholars of England to make one Bible, which the Church shall be bound to, out of all the Bibles that men use.'

'*I* knew.' Ben could not lift his eyes from the printed page. 'I'm more about Court than you think. The learning of Oxford and Cambridge – ''most noble and most equal'', as I have said – and Westminster, to sit upon a clutch of Bibles. Those 'ud be Geneva (my mother read to me out of it at her knee), Douai, Rheims, Coverdale, Matthew's, the Bishops', the Great, and so forth.'

'They are all set down on the page there – text against text. And you call me a botcher of old clothes?'

'Justly. But what's your concern with this botchery? To keep peace among the Divines? There's fifty of 'em at it as I've heard.'

'I deal with but one. He came to know me when we played at Oxford – when the plague was too hot in London.'

'I remember this Miles Smith now. Son of a butcher? Hey?' Ben grunted.

'Is it so?' was the quiet answer. 'He was moved, he said, with some lines of mine in Dick's part. He said they were, to his godly apprehension, a parable, as it might be, of his reverend self, going down darkling to his tomb 'twixt cliffs of ice and iron.'

'What lines? I know none of thine of that power. But in my *Sejanus* – '

'These were in my *Macbeth*. They lost nothing at Dick's mouth:–

>   To-morrow, and to-morrow, and to-morrow
>   Creeps in this petty pace from day to day
>   To the last syllable of recorded time,
>   And all our yesterdays have lighted fools
>   The way to dusty death –

or something in that sort. Condell writes 'em out fair for him, and tells him I am Justice of the Peace (wherein he lied) and *armiger*, which brings me within the pale of God's creatures and the Church. Little and little, then, this very reverend Miles Smith opens his mind to me. He and a half-score others, his cloth, are cast to furbish up the Prophets – Isaiah to Malachi. In his opinion by what he'd heard, I had some skill in words, and he'd condescend – '

'How?' Ben barked. 'Condescend?'

'Why not? He'd condescend to inquire o' me privily, when direct illumination lacked, for a tricking-out of his words or the turn of some figure. For example' – Will pointed to the papers – 'here be the first three verses of the Sixtieth of Isaiah, and the nineteenth and twentieth of that same. Miles has been at a stand over 'em a week or more.'

'They never called on *me*.' Ben caressed lovingly the hand-pressed proofs on their lavish linen paper. 'Here's the Latin atop and' – his thick forefinger ran down the slip – 'some three – four – Englishings out of the other Bibles. They spare 'emselves nothing. Let's to it together. Will you have the Latin first?'

'Could I choke ye from that, Holofernes?'

Ben rolled forth, richly: ' "*Surge, illumare, Jerusalem, quia venit lumen tuum, et gloria Domini super te orta est. Quia ecce tenebrae operient terram et caligo populos. Super te autem orietur Dominus, et gloria ejus in te videbitur. Et ambulabunt gentes in lumine tuo, et reges in splendore ortus tui.*" Er-hum? Think you to better that?'

'How have Smith's crew gone about it?'

'Thus.' Ben read from the paper. ' "Get thee up, O Jerusalem, and be bright, for thy light is at hand, and the glory of God has risen up upon thee." '

'Up-pup-up!' Will stuttered profanely.

Ben held on. ' "See how darkness is upon the earth and the peoples thereof." '

'That's no great stuff to put into Isaiah's mouth. And further, Ben?'

' "But on thee God shall shew light and on – " or "in," is

it?' (Ben held the proof closer to the deep furrow at the bridge of his nose.) ' "On thee shall His glory be manifest. So that all peoples shall walk in thy light and the Kings in the glory of thy morning." '

'It may be mended. Read me the Coverdale of it now. 'Tis on the same sheet – to the right, Ben.'

'Umm – umm! Coverdale saith, "And therefore get thee up betimes, for thy light cometh, and the glory of the Lord shall rise up upon thee. For lo! while the darkness and cloud covereth the earth and the people, the Lord shall shew thee light, and His glory shall be seen in thee. The Gentiles shall come to thy light, and kings to the brightness that springeth forth upon thee." But "gentes" is, for the most part, "peoples",' Ben concluded.

'Eh?' said Will indifferently. 'Art sure?'

This loosed an avalanche of instances from Ovid, Quintilian, Terence, Columella, Seneca, and others. Will took no heed till the rush ceased, but stared into the orchard, through the September haze. 'Now give me the Douai and Geneva for this "Get thee up, O Jerusalem",' said he at last. 'They'll be all there.'

Ben referred to the proofs. ''Tis "arise" in both,' said he. ' "Arise and be bright" in Geneva. In the Douai 'tis "Arise and be illuminated".'

'So? Give me the paper now.' Will took it from his companion, rose, and paced towards a tree in the orchard, turning again, when he had reached it, by a well-worn track through the grass. Ben leaned forward in his chair. The other's free hand went up warningly.

'Quiet, man!' said he. 'I wait on my Demon!' He fell into the stage-stride of his art at that time, speaking to the air.

'How shall this open? "Arise?" No! "Rise!" Yes. And we'll have no weak coupling. 'Tis a call to a City! "Rise – shine" . . . Nor yet any schoolmaster's "because" – because Isaiah is not Holofernes. "*Rise – shine; for thy light is come, and – !*" ' He refreshed himself from the apple and the proofs as he strode. ' "And – and the glory of God!" – No! "God" 's over short. We need the long roll here. "*And the glory of the*

Lord is risen on thee.'' (Isaiah speaks the part. We'll have it from his own lips.) What's next in Smith's stuff? . . . ''See how?'' Oh, vile – vile! . . . And Geneva hath ''Lo''? (Still, Ben! Still!) ''Lo'' is better by all odds: but to match the long roll of ''the Lord'' we'll have it ''Behold''. How goes it now? *For, behold, darkness clokes the earth and –* and – '' What's the colour and use of this cursed *caligo,* Ben? – ''*Et caligo populos''.*'

' ''Mistiness'' or, as in Pliny, ''blindness''. And further – '

'No – o . . . Maybe, though, *caligo* will piece out *tenebrae.* ''*Quia ecce tenebrae operient terram et caligo populos.''* Nay! ''Shadow'' and ''mist'' are not men enough for this work . . . Blindness, did ye say, Ben? . . . The blackness of blindness atop of mere darkness? . . . By God, I've used it in my own stuff many times! ''Gross'' searches it to the hilts! ''Darkness covers'' – no – ''clokes'' (short always). ''*Darkness clokes the earth, and gross – gross darkness the people!''* (But Isaiah's prophesying, with the storm behind him. Can ye not *feel* it, Ben? It must be ''shall'') – ''*Shall cloke the earth''* . . . The rest comes clearer . . . ''But on thee God shall arise'' . . . (Nay, that's sacrificing the Creator to the Creature!) ''*But the Lord shall arise on thee,''* and – yes, we'll sound that ''thee'' again – ''and on thee shall'' – No! . . . ''*And His glory shall be seen on thee.''* Good!' He walked his beat a little in silence, mumbling the two verses before he mouthed them.

'I have it! Heark, Ben! ''*Rise – shine; for thy light is come, and the glory of the Lord is risen on thee. For, behold, darkness shall cloke the earth, and gross darkness the people. But the Lord shall arise on thee, and His glory shall be seen upon thee.''* '

'There's something not all amiss there,' Ben conceded.

'My Demon never betrayed me yet, while I trusted him. Now for the verse that runs to the blast of rams'–horns. ''*Et ambulabunt gentes in lumine tuo, et reges in splendore ortus tui.''* How goes that in the Smithy? ''The Gentiles shall come to thy light, and kings to the brightness that springs forth upon thee?'' The same in Coverdale and the Bishops' – eh? We'll keep ''Gentiles'', Ben, for the sake of the indraught of the last syllable. But it might be "And the Gentiles shall draw". No! The plainer the better! "The Gentiles shall come to thy light, and kings to the splendour of – " (Smith's out here! We'll need something that shall lift the trumpet anew.) "Kings shall – shall – Kings to – " (Listen, Ben, but on your life speak not!) "Gentiles shall come to thy light, and kings to thy brightness" – No! "Kings to the brightness that springeth – " Serves not! . . . One trumpet must answer another. And the blast of a trumpet is always *ai-ai*. "The brightness of" – "*Ortus*" signifies "rising", Ben – or what?'

'Ay, or "birth", or the East in general.'

'Ass! 'Tis the one word that answers to "light". "Kings to the brightness of thy rising." Look! The thing shines now within and without. God! That so much should lie on a word!' He repeated the verse – ' "*And the Gentiles shall come to thy light, and kings to the brightness of thy rising.*" '

He walked to the table and wrote rapidly on the proof margin all three verses as he had spoken them. 'If they hold by this,' said he, raising his head, 'they'll not go far astray. Now for the nineteenth and twentieth verses. On the other sheet, Ben. What? What? Smith says he has held back his rendering till he hath seen mine? Then we'll botch 'em as they stand. Read me first the Latin; next the Coverdale, and last the Bishops'. There's a contagion of sleep in the air.' He handed back the proofs, yawned, and took up his walk.

Obedient, Ben began: ' "*Non erit tibi amplius Sol ad lucendum per diem, nec splendor Lunae illuminabit te.*" Which Coverdale rendereth, "The Sun shall never be thy day light, and the light of the Moon shall never shine unto thee." The Bishops read: "Thy sun shall never be thy daylight and the light of the moon shall never shine on thee." '

'Coverdale is the better,' said Will, and, wrinkling his nose a little, 'The Bishops put out their lights clumsily. Have at it, Ben.'

Ben pursed his lips and knit his brow. 'The two verses are in the same mode, changing a hand's-breadth in the second. By so much, therefore, the more difficult.'

'Ye see *that*, then?' said the other, staring past him, and

muttering as he paced, concerning suns and moons. Presently
he took back the proof, chose him another apple, and grunted.
'Umm – umm! "Thy Sun shall never be – " No! Flat as a
split viol. "*Non erit tibi amplius Sol – *" That *amplius* must
give tongue. Ah! . . . "Thy Sun shall not – shall not – shall
no more be thy light by day" . . . A fair entry. "Nor?"
– No! Not on the heels of "day". "Neither" it must be –
"Neither the Moon" – but here's *splendor* and the rams-horns
again. (Therefore – *ai – ai!*) "Neither for brightness shall the
Moon – " (Pest! It is the Lord who is taking the Moon's place
over Israel. It must be "thy Moon".) "Neither for brightness
shall thy Moon light – give – make – give light unto thee."
Ah! . . . Listen here! . . . "*The Sun shall no more be thy
light by day: neither for brightness shall thy Moon give light
unto thee.*" That serves, and more, for the first entry. What
next, Ben?'

Ben nodded magisterially as Will neared him, reached out
his hand for the proofs, and read: ' "*Sed erit tibi Dominus
in lucem sempiternam et Deus tuus in gloriam tuam.*" Here
is a jewel of Coverdale's that the Bishops have wisely stolen
whole. Hear! "*But* the Lord Himself shall be thy everlasting
light, and thy God shall be thy glory." ' Ben paused. 'There's
a hand's-breadth of splendour for a simple man to gather!'

'Both hands rather. He's swept the strings as divinely as
David before Saul,' Will assented. 'We'll convey it whole, too
. . . What's amiss now, Holofernes?'

For Ben was regarding him with a scholar's cold pity. 'Both
hands! Will, hast thou *ever* troubled to master *any* shape or
sort of prosody – the mere names of the measures and pulses
of strung words?'

'I beget some such stuff and send it to you to christen.
What's your wisdomhood in labour of?'

'Naught. Naught. But not to know the names of the tools
of his trade!' Ben half muttered and pronounced some Greek
word or other which conveyed nothing to the listener, who
replied: 'Pardon, then, for whatever sin it was. I do but know
words for my need of 'em, Ben. Hold still awhile!'

He went back to his pacings and mutterings. ' "For the Lord

Himself shall be thy – or thine? – everlasting light." Yes. We'll
convey that.' He repeated it twice. 'Nay! Can be bettered. Hark
ye, Ben. Here is the Sun going up to over-run and possess all
Heaven for evermore. *There*fore (Still, man!) we'll harness the
horses of the dawn. Hear their hooves? "The Lord Himself shall
be unto thee thy everlasting light, and – " Hold again! After
that climbing thunder must be some smooth check – like great
wings gliding. *There*fore we'll not have "shall be thy glory",
but "*And* thy God thy glory!" Ay – even as an eagle alighteth!
Good – good! Now again, the sun and moon of that twentieth
verse, Ben.'

Ben read: ' "*Non occidet ultra Sol tuus et Luna tua non
minuetur: quia erit tibi Dominus in lucem sempiternam et
complebuntur dies luctus tui.*" '

Will snatched the paper and read aloud from the Coverdale
version. ' "Thy Sun shall never go down, and thy Moon shall
not be taken away . . . " What a plague's Coverdale doing with
his blocking *ets* and *urs*, Ben? What's *minuetur*? . . . I'll have
it all anon.'

'Minish – make less - appease – abate, as in – '

'So?' . . . Will threw the proofs back. 'Then "wane" should
serve. "Neither shall thy moon wane" . . . "Wane" is good,
but over-weak for place next to "moon" ' . . . He swore softly.
'Isaiah hath abolished both earthly sun and moon. *Exeunt
ambo*. Aha! I begin to see! . . . Sol, the man, goes down
– down stairs or trap – as needs be. Therefore "Go down"
shall stand. "Set" would have been better – as a sword sent
home in the scabbard – but it jars – it jars. Now Luna must
retire herself in some simple fashion . . . Which? Ass that
I be! 'Tis common talk in all the plays . . . "Withdrawn"
. . . "Favour withdrawn" . . . "Countenance withdrawn".
"The Queen withdraws herself" . . . "Withdraw", it shall be!
"Neither shall thy moon withdraw herself." (Hear her silver
train rasp the boards, Ben?) "*Thy sun shall no more go down
– neither shall thy moon withdraw herself. For the Lord . . .*"
– ay, the Lord, simple of Himself – "*shall be thine*" – yes,
"thine" here – "*everlasting light, and*" . . . How goes the
ending, Ben?'

' "*Et complebuntur dies luctus tui.*" ' Ben read. ' "And thy sorrowful days shall be rewarded thee," says Coverdale.'

'And the Bishops?'

' "And thy sorrowful days shall be ended." '

'By no means. And Douai?'

' "Thy sorrow shall be ended." '

'And Geneva?'

' "And the days of thy mourning shall be ended." '

'The Switzers have it! Lay the tail of Geneva to the head of Coverdale and the last is without flaw.' He began to thump Ben on the shoulder. 'We have it! I have it all, Boanerges! Blessed be my Demon! Hear! "*The sun shall no more be thy light by day, neither for brightness the moon by night. But the Lord Himself shall be unto thee thy everlasting light, and thy God thy glory.*" ' He drew a deep breath and went on. ' "*Thy sun shall no more go down; neither shall thy moon withdraw herself, for the Lord shall be thine everlasting light, and the days of thy mourning shall be ended.*" ' The rain of triumphant blows began again. 'If those other seven devils in London let it stand on this sort, it serves. But God knows what they can *not* turn upsee-dejee!'

Ben wriggled. 'Let be!' he protested. 'Ye are more moved by this jugglery than if the Globe were burned.'

'Thatch – old thatch! And full of fleas! . . . But, Ben, ye should have heard my Ezekiel making mock of fallen Tyrus in his twenty-seventh chapter. Miles sent me the whole, for, he said, some small touches. I took it to the Bank – four o'clock of a summer morn; stretched out in one of our wherries – and watched London, Port and Town, up and down the river, waking all arrayed to heap more upon evident excess. Ay! "A merchant for the peoples of many isles" . . . "The ships of Tarshish did sing of thee in thy markets"? Yes! I saw all Tyre before me neighing her pride against lifted heaven . . . But what will they let stand of all mine at long last? Which? I'll never know.'

He had set himself neatly and quickly to refolding and cording the packet while he talked. 'That's secret enough,' he said at the finish.

'He'll lose it by the way.' Ben pointed to the sleeper beneath the tree. 'He's owl-drunk.'

'But not his horse,' said Will. He crossed the orchard, roused the man; slid the packet into an holster which he carefully rebuckled; saw him out of the gate, and returned to his chair.

'Who will know we had part in it?' Ben asked.

'God, maybe – if He ever lay ear to earth. I've gained and lost enough – lost enough.' He lay back and sighed. There was long silence till he spoke half aloud. 'And Kit that was my master in the beginning, he died when all the world was young.'

'Knifed on a tavern reckoning – not even for a wench!' Ben nodded.

'Ay. But if he'd lived he'd have breathed me! 'Fore God, he'd have breathed me!'

'Was Marlowe, or any man, *ever* thy master, Will?'

'He alone. Very he. I envied Kit. Ye do not know that envy, Ben?'

'Not as touching my own works. When the mob is led to prefer a baser Muse, I have felt the hurt, and paid home. Ye know that – as ye know my doctrine of play-writing.'

'Nay – not wholly – tell it at large,' said Will, relaxing in his seat, for virtue had gone out of him. He put a few drowsy questions. In three minutes Ben had launched full-flood on the decayed state of the drama, which he was born to correct; on cabals and intrigues against him which he had fought without cease; and on the inveterate muddle-headedness of the mob unless duly scourged into approbation by his magisterial hand.

It was very still in the orchard now that the horse had gone. The heat of the day held though the sun sloped, and the wine had done its work. Presently, Ben's discourse was broken by a snort from the other chair.

'I was listening, Ben! Missed not a word – missed not a word.' Will sat up and rubbed his eyes. 'Ye held me throughout.' His head dropped again before he had done speaking.

Ben looked at him with a chuckle and quoted from one of his own plays:–

'Mine earnest vehement botcher
And deacon also, Will, I cannot dispute with you.'

He drew out flint, steel and tinder, pipe and tobacco-bag
from somewhere round his waist, lit and puffed against the
midges till he, too, dozed.

NOTES

The following Notes are not intended to be exhaustive. Scrupulous annotation of 'The Last of the Stories', for instance, would run to several pages of names, dates and works of the writers alluded to, without for the most part offering readers anything that wasn't self-explanatory or that they didn't know already. What I have therefore aimed to provide is information about initial publication, brief details and comments that seem enlightening or helpful, and suggestions for further reading where appropriate.

The Last of the Stories   Page 1

First published in *The Week's News*, September 15th, 1888; republished in *Abaft the Funnel* (1909), an unauthorised American collection; collected in the Sussex Edition (1937-9) vol. xxix. (This thirty-five volume de luxe edition was personally supervised by Kipling before his death in 1936 and still constitutes the nearest approach to a definitive edition of his work.)

To make a story out of being taken to a 'Limbo of Lost Endeavour, where the souls of all the Characters go' is a typically Kiplingesque notion. He later produced equally unorthodox versions of Heaven in 'On the Gate' (*Debits and Credits*) and of Purgatory in 'Uncovenanted Mercies' (*Limits and Renewals*). The very idea of such a Limbo and of meeting your own characters (who then tell you that you didn't understand them) is of course a perfect example of how to make a story out of not having a story to tell. This itself is a variation on the familiar Romantic formula of 'this is what I should write if only I could', as well as being an anticipation of the kind of literary self-consciousness much practised by writers in this century. None of which should disguise the fact that Kipling is here plainly the young author keen to show off both the range of his reading (Dante, Rabelais, Balzac, Gautier, Zola, and a whole host of more recent British and American writers) and the extent of his own already sizeable literary output. The exuberantly arch tone of the story is thoroughly characteristic of much of Kipling's early Indian work.

L'Envoi   Page 15

First published as the epilogue to *Life's Handicap* (1891).

When he came to republish this as a separate poem, Kipling changed the title to 'My New-Cut Ashlar', radically altered the punctuation and transposed verses four and five. This is the text of the poem as it first appeared. The pseudo-Biblical manner is one that Kipling used extensively in his middle and later work, usually in poems on public occasions like 'Recessional'.

'The Finest Story in the World'   Page 17

First published in *The Contemporary Review*, July 1891 and collected in *Many Inventions* (1893).

It is not easy to decide where to place the main emphasis of this story. Is it simply a story of metempsychosis? A North London version of Wordsworth's 'Immortality Ode'? How a nine-to-five job and the first awakenings of sexual love destroy the capacity to recall past lives? Or is is really far less about Charlie Mears, the young poetaster-bank clerk, and far more about the narrator's misguided attempt to pull off a great metaphysical/literary coup?

On quite a different level the story shows Kipling's early infatuation with America. The narrator encourages Charlie to read Longfellow and Charlie himself 're-experiences' moments from *Eirik's Saga* (which contains an account of the first Viking landings on the coast of North America). Kipling had read the Icelandic Songs in William Morris's translations. American poetry he had discovered at school and not only Longfellow but also Walt Whitman whose free verse seems to lie behind Charlie's so-called 'blank verse' about the galley slaves. To find Kipling writing such a fine piece of free verse may at first seem surprising. After all, doesn't he recall in his autobiography, *Something of Myself*, how he 'plus some Chianti' once told W. E. Henley, another early exponent, that 'free verse was like fishing with barbless hooks'? In fact, Kipling experimented with most of the available poetic forms and this is by no means his only successful excursion into free verse.

When 'Omer Smote 'Is Bloomin' Lyre   Page 47

First published as the untitled, prefatory poem to the second series of 'Barrack-Room Ballads' in *The Seven Seas* (1896).

Subsequently the poem has always appeared, as here, with the first line as title. Kipling's nonchalant acknowledgement that he and all writers are basically thieves would of course lose all its edge and a good deal of its point, if instead of being written in Cockney the poem had been written in standard English.

A Letter to the *Spectator*   Page 48

Originally published in the Letters section of the *Spectator* on July 2nd, 1898; subsequently collected with the added subtitle 'Shakespeare and *THE TEMPEST*' in the Sussex Edition vol. xxx. This virtually unknown piece is the first of Kipling's imaginative reconstructions of how Shakespeare might have gathered starting points for his plays (see also 'The Craftsman'). Kipling himself was famous for 'pumping' chance acquaintance in just this way.

'Wireless'   Page 52

First published in *Scribner's Magazine*, August 1902 and collected in *Traffics and Discoveries* (1904).

Like many of his stories, this shows Kipling's fascination with new technology and also his ability to make use of it for metaphorical purposes. Here radio transmission serves as a metaphor for how poetic inspiration occurs. Shaynor, the young, consumptive chemist's assistant, under quasi-Keatsian conditions, involuntarily produces partial versions of 'The Eve of St Agnes' and 'Ode to a Nightingale' – though only partial, since as the story suggests he is a 'faulty receiver', capable merely of getting 'a word here and there'. This idea that inspiration is involuntary and comes from without was one of Kipling's most deeply-held literary beliefs: 'We are only telephone wires', he told Rider Haggard in 1918. J. M. S. Tompkins in *The Art of Rudyard Kipling* (1959) provides the most helpful discussion of the story.

Literature   Page 72

This speech was originally delivered at the annual Royal Academy Dinner on May 5th, 1906. When Kipling later collected it with thirty-one other speeches in *A Book of Words* (1928), he added the epigraph:

I am Earth, overtaking all things except words. They alone
escape me. Therefore I lie heavy on their makers.

During the course of the speech Kipling quizzes his audience on the identity of six unnamed writers 'afflicted with the magic of the necessary word': the 'tinker in Bedford gaol'; the 'pamphleteering shopkeeper, pilloried in London'; the 'muzzy Scot'; the 'despised German Jew'; the 'condemned French thief'; and the 'English Admiralty official'. One wonders how many correctly identified John Bunyan, Daniel Defoe, Robert Burns, Heinrich Heine, François Villon and Samuel Pepys.

And what did the audience make of the two Just So-like parables that begin and end the speech? The first seems plain enough: literature satisfies a basic human and social need though it is not without its dangers for those who dare to´ record 'the tale of the Tribe'. But what of the second, concluding parable about the Tribe and the failure of its rain-doctors to produce well-regulated rain? *The Times* report on the speech (published on May 7th) takes it for granted that the point of the parable is entirely literary: countries get the literature they deserve. With hindsight I suspect one can see rather more to it. Six months before in December 1905 a Liberal Ministry had come to power after years of Tory rule and consolidated its position with a large majority in the General Election held in January 1906. (According to *The Times* report, the new Liberal Prime Minister, Sir Henry Campbell-Bannerman, was amongst Kipling's audience and had himself delivered a short speech.) The point of the parable is therefore as much political as literary: countries not only get the literature they deserve but the government too. And the reason that England has now got a Liberal Government is, in Kipling's terms, because 'our head-men have been running about hunting jackals, and our little people have been running about chasing grasshoppers!' Incidentally, this landslide Liberal victory represented almost the final blow to Kipling's own hopes of a new brand of Empire-based Conservatism which he had persuaded himself might replace the self-satisfied inertia of the Tory old guard. Although he was always to remain passionately interested in politics, the year 1906 in effect marks the end of Kipling's rampantly jingoistic period.

The Fabulists   Page 76

First published in *A Diversity of Creatures* (1917).

What is perhaps most striking about this poem (apart from a riddling quality unusual in his verse) are the explicit references in the final stanza to the First World War. It is this sudden shift to the present, together with the implied reminder that Kipling had been predicting such catastrophe for years, that give a particular resonance to the poem's generalities about the problems facing the artist.

The Craftsman   Page 78

First published in *The Years Between* (1919).·

Like 'A Letter to the *Spectator*' this offers another of Kipling's deliberately 'unofficial' versions of how Shakespeare might have

derived hints for his plays. More remarkably, 'The Craftsman' is
one of the very few successful poems in English written in Sapphics.
Kipling probably tried the experiment as a result of his lifelong
interest in Horace (see Note to 'The Survival') but his admiration
for Swinburne who also wrote Sapphics may have played its part.
Those who wish to find out more about Horatian measures will find
an informative account in J. B. Leishman's *Translating Horace* (1956)
and a brief but handy discussion in G. S. Fraser's *Metre, Rhyme and
Free Verse* (1970).

The Bull That Thought   Page 80
First published in *MacLean's Magazine*, November 1924 and
Cosmopolitan Magazine, December 1924; collected in *Debits and
Credits* (1926).

This story is one of Kipling's most powerful allegories about art
and the artist, providing amongst other things a subtly transposed
version of his own career from early prodigy to late (neglected)
master. According to *The Readers' Guide to Rudyard Kipling's
Work* (1961-72), Kipling may have found a hint for his story of
Apis (named after the Egyptian bull god) in the career of Lechuzo,
a bull who in 1890 fought so well in the ring that contrary to custom
he wasn't killed after the fights. Eventually a rich Andalusian bought
Lechuzo and took him to live on his farm. There are perceptive
discussions of the story and its different levels of meaning in C. A.
Bodelsen's *Aspects of Kipling's Art* (1964) and in Elliot L. Gilbert's
The Good Kipling (1972).

Fiction   Page 96
This speech was originally delivered to the Royal Literary Society on
July 7th, 1926. It appeared under the title 'The Art of Fiction' in *The
Times* the following day and was published in pamphlet form later
the same year. When he came to collect the speech in *A Book of
Words* (1928), Kipling called the speech simply 'Fiction', misdated
its delivery as June and added the following epigraph:
Gold and Gems we may steal – melt down, re-cut and re-sell them.
   All that we need is the Fire. That we must find in ourselves.
Reading this speech now, one is struck I think by two things. The
first is how vigorously Swift's reputation has reasserted itself since
Kipling's description of it in the mid 1920s. The second is the way
in which a number of Kipling's observations anticipate the kind of
statements that T. S. Eliot and others were to turn into critical

commonplaces over the succeeding decades. In the Introduction I gave as one example of this his remark about authorial intention. Another would be his comment that 'In every age some men gain temporary favour because they happen to have met a temporary need of their age.' This interestingly anticipates Eliot's (somewhat acid) observation in 'Thoughts After Lambeth' (1931) that 'when I wrote a poem called *The Waste Land* some of the more approving critics said that I had expressed the "disillusionment of a generation", which is nonsense. I may have expressed for them their illusion of being disillusioned, but that did not form part of my intention.' The tone of course is quite different but the basic point is remarkably similar.

The Survival   Page 100
First published in *Debits and Credits* (1926)

This is not, as it claims to be, a translation of Horace's Ode 22, Bk V at all; it is an original poem by Kipling. Horace never wrote a Fifth Book of Odes, although a volume entitled *Q. Horati Flacci Carminum Liber Quintus a Rudyardo Kipling et Carolo Graves Anglice Redditus* was published in 1920. This literary hoax was the work of Kipling, Charles Graves (brother of Robert), A. D. Godley and others. The idea seems to have arisen from two earlier 'Horatian' poems of Kipling's, 'The Pro-Consuls' (1905) and 'A Translation' (published 1917 but probably written as early as 1908). After the appearance of *Q. Horati Flacci Carminum Liber Quintus*, Kipling seems to have sensed more serious possibilities in this kind of 'translation' and wrote four further 'Odes' from this 'Fifth Book', including 'The Survival', and published them in *Debits and Credits*. These later 'Odes' offer Kipling a mask not dissimilar from the one Ezra Pound adopts in a poem like 'Homage to Sextus Propertius'. A full account of Kipling's lifelong preoccupation with Horace is given in Charles Carrington's *Kipling's Horace* (1978).

A Legend of Truth   Page 101
First published in *Debits and Credits* (1926).

These versatile couplets share something of the tone and parabolic character of 'Literature' and 'Fiction'. From a more technical point of view, they show how effectively Kipling can play off the consciously poetic archaism of 'Besought me for my useful tongue or pen' against the urgent, telegrammatic modernity of 'Come at once. Facts out of hand.' Underlying the poem is a strong sense of Kipling's own need to return to fiction after the years spent on *The Irish Guards in the*

Great War (1923), an official history he undertook as a memorial to his only son John who served with the Irish Guards and was killed in October 1915.

Dayspring Mishandled   Page 103

First published in *McCall's Magazine*, March 1928 and in *Strand Magazine*, July 1928; collected in *Limits and Renewals* (1932).

This dark masterpiece of abortive literary revenge is characteristic of Kipling's highly condensed, elliptical, later manner. It is also an example of how in these later stories he will rework at greater length and with far greater psychological depth elements from much earlier stories. This one, for instance, looks back over forty years to 'Pig' from his first collection *Plain Tales from the Hills* (1888), which similarly enacts a kind of scholastic revenge.

In the Introduction I referred to Kipling's unconventional use of literary allusions. The early stories were often prefaced by a brief epigraph (unacknowledged but usually by Kipling himself), a practise he derived from earlier nineteenth century fiction. In the later work he extended this technique by bracketing his stories with poems which obliquely comment on the stories they surround. Here he returns to the use of a cryptic but highly suggestive epigraph taken from 'La Fée aux Miettes' by the French Romantic writer Charles Nodier (1780-1844). The story also contains that very Nineties refrain 'I have been faithful to thee, Cynara! in my fashion' from Ernest Dowson's poem 'Non sum qualis eram bonae sub regno Cynarae'. Given the time frame of the story, one might have expected Dowson but the presence of Nodier is I think a genuine surprise. Kipling's reading was nothing if not eclectic and his deployment of it often extremely apt. The most helpful discussions of the story are to be found in J. M. S. Tompkin's book and in Angus Wilson's *The Strange Ride of Rudyard Kipling* (1977).

Gertrude's Prayer   Page 124

These verses were added to 'Dayspring Mishandled' as a kind of coda when Kipling collected the story in *Limits and Renewals*.

In addition to extending the story's sense of textual uncertainty (why 'modernised'? 'modernised' by whom? etc), the verses can be read as a comment on the emotional and imaginative distortions that have 'wried and knotted' Manallace's personality and talent. That Manallace himself is supposed to have written them only intensifies the irony.

'Proofs of Holy Writ'   Page 125

First published in *Strand Magazine*, April 1934 and collected in the Sussex Edition vol. xxx.

This very late, relatively unknown story does considerably more than posit the engaging hypothesis that Shakespeare had a hand in parts of the King James Bible. It presents an absorbing account of the 'Kipling writer' at work, waiting on his 'Demon', sifting and adapting material in search of the 'necessary word'. Kipling found support for his belief that inspiration was involuntary and came from without in the Classical Greek notion of a personal Daemon who would at times take control of a writer's imagination. In *Something of Myself* he advises young would-be authors: 'When your Daemon is in charge, do not try to think consciously. Drift, wait, and obey.' Here Kipling's Daemon even goes so far as to produce an 'improved' Authorised version of the verses from Isaiah, as one can see by comparing the epigraph with the 'Shakespearean' version. The story's punning title comes of course from *Othello* III, iii, 321.

Other titles in **THE ENCORE SERIES** published by **Tabb House**

All titles 205 x 135mm.

This series brings neglected traditional writing and classics to the attention of the modern reader, and for the first three titles, paintings by Caeria Strong (Israel) were specially commissioned.
'High quality productions; elegant yet economical editions ideal for both students and the general reader' Publishing News

THE HAUNTING *by* **C. A. Dawson Scott.** *Foreword by* **Francis King**
Mrs Dawson Scott's novel of paranormal suspense, set in a small Cornish port (Padstow) in the 19th century, makes compelling reading.
'The narrative has imaginative power; I recommend this as a late night solitary read' *Literary Review*
248 pp. Hbk. £8.50. Sewn pbk. £3.95.

MALACHI'S COVE and Other Stories and Essays *by* **Anthony Trollope**
Edited with an Introduction by **Richard Mullen**
Travelling and the writing of fiction form the theme of this volume and the reader is taken from Cornwall to Ireland, France and America.
'Doctor Mullen has done a considerable service in selecting some of Trollope's best short stories' *Contemporary Review*
'A handsomely produced book – worthy in every way to stand beside the Barchester novels' *Church Times*
168 pp. Hbk. £7.95. Sewn pbk. £3.50.

ONE POOR SCRUPLE *by* **Mrs Wilfrid Ward.** *Introduction by* **Bernard Bergonzi**
London society life at the turn of the century and the moral conflicts of the protagonists provide the setting and the cause of dramatic interest in this leisurely novel.
'Powerful, haunting and beautiful' *Journal of Pre-Raphaelite Studies.*
400 pp. Hbk. £8.95. Sewn pbk. £3.95

Published in 1989

KIPLING'S LOST WORLD: Selected Writings *by* **Rudyard Kipling**
Edited and with an Introduction by **Harry Ricketts**
This collection of poems, stories, letters and speeches offers a mixture of well-known, lesser known and virtually unknown pieces, from every decade of Kipling's writing life, from the 1880s to the 1930s. The arrangement of the pieces in chronological order allows the reader to experience the development of Kipling's ideas on art, his sense of the value of literature and his opinions about the literary life itself.
   How literature is created, how literary talent can be corrupted or misapplied, hypotheses for how poetic inspiration occurs, how Shakespeare might have gathered material for *The Tempest*, and the irony that art survives the civilisation which begat it: these themes and conundrums are presented with that immediacy and ability to buttonhole the reader that has ever been the hallmark of Kipling's writing.
Cover portrait of Rudyard Kipling by William Strang. Pbk £4.95. Hbk £10.95.